Rebuilding Social Capital

Maryann O. Keating

Barry P. Keating

ACTONINSTITUTE
Christian Social Thought Series
Number 28 • Edited by Kevin Schmiesing

Christian Social Thought Series, Number 28

© 2020 by Acton Institute

Acton Institute
for the Study of Religion and Liberty
All rights reserved.

Cover image: Group of people on peak mountain climbing helping team work, travel trekking success business concept
Source: www.istock.com

ISBN: 978-1-880595-25-1

Interior composition: Judy Schafer
Cover: Peter Ho

ACTON INSTITUTE

98 E. Fulton
Grand Rapids, Michigan 49503
616.454.3080
www.acton.org

Printed in the United States of America

Contents

I	Introduction	1
II	The Concept of Social Capital	3
III	Opportunities to Practice and Gain Social Capital	13
IV	Declines in Voluntary, Civic, and Religious Participation	21
V	Linking Social Capital with Participation in Organizations	41
VI	Requirements for Growth in Social Capital	55
VII	Reawakening a Vibrant Civic Sector	65
References		79
About the Authors		83

1 Introduction*

Robert Putnam, an American political scientist best known for his books *Bowling Alone* and *Our Kids*, believes that the performance of government and other social institutions is powerfully influenced by citizen engagement in the public square. He, along with other social scientists, labels the capabilities fostered by such engagement as *social capital*, the capacity for groups to form and pursue shared objectives.[1]

Putnam is not merely nostalgic but seriously concerned about issues affecting civil society. Other social philosophers similarly identify a decline in social capital as a primary issue affecting contemporary governance. Following the breakdown of the Soviet Union in 1988, it was generally accepted that the former Soviet bloc countries lacked a well-developed civil society. Recent research, however, has focused on the decline in social capital in economically advanced countries, including

---

* We wish to thank Craig Ladwig of the Indiana Policy Review Foundation and the Dekko Foundation for encouraging us to examine the role of voluntary organizations in creating social capital. We also wish to acknowledge the help of Kevin Schmiesing, the editor of this publication for the Acton Institute. Any shortcomings remain our own.

[1] Robert D. Putnam, *Bowling Alone: The Collapse and Revival of American Community* (New York: Simon & Schuster, 2000); idem, Our Kids: The American Dream in Crisis (New York: Simon & Schuster, 2015).

the United States—a phenomenon that has been called the "Great Disruption."

We hypothesize that a decline in the ability to work toward common objectives is a symptom of declining opportunities for individuals to acquire social capital throughout their lives. To determine whether Americans spend less time on accumulating social capital, we consider the amount of time households and, in particular, teenagers spend participating in voluntary, religious, and social activities. Our goal is to identify factors disrupting the formation of social capital and participation in private organizations, a hallmark of American culture.

Economic terms such as the Great Depression, capital stock (e.g., machinery, tools, equipment, and technical know-how), and externalities are appropriated in our work to describe social phenomena. Economists study and write extensively on maintaining free enterprise in the public square, and, we suggest, some of these concepts transfer in understanding civil society. Economic freedom, after all, is only one element of human freedom.[2]

A significant difference between economic and overall social wellbeing is that declines in economic production and a nation's capital stock are explicit and capture widespread attention. Of greater importance is the less measurable loss in social capital.

Does it make a difference if social capital is diminishing? On a practical level, significant public resources are needed to pick up the slack when individuals do not share a working consensus on rights and responsibilities. Furthermore, if a critical mass of individuals fails to follow social norms, then the government, to maintain order, is required to become more coercive and intrusive. Quality of life, constitutional democracy, and markets function only when they can live off several centuries of accumulated social capital.

---

[2] See Pope John Paul II, Encyclical Letter *Centesimus Annus* (1991), no. 39. Hereafter cited as CA.

II The Concept of Social Capital

Social capital refers to a certain set of informal values and skills shared among members of a group that permit cooperation regardless of socioeconomic characteristics. Social capital can be directed toward harmful ends but, for now, we define *social capital* as the learned ability of individuals to engage socially and work within organizations to pursue common objectives.

In economics, the term "fixed capital" refers to a stock of equipment, and investment and depreciation are flows adding to or decreasing the existing stock. The stock of social capital at any point in time is fixed but may be augmented or diminished by changing institutions and the behavior of residents. A significant factor responsible for the Great Disruption in social capital is a loss of transcendental religious beliefs maintaining the social order. Without religious sanctions or some other code of ethics sustaining traditional attachments and responsibilities, the stock of social capital declines.

Catholic Social Teaching and Social Capital

Catholic social teaching (CST) offers hope to those concerned with maintaining social order in a democratic state. Ultimately, it provides a framework available to all for sustaining traditional attachments and responsibilities along with personal autonomy.

Catholic social teaching deals explicitly with the positive value of voluntary associations and thus indirectly with social capital. John Paul II is forthright about the interest of the Church, as just one of many voluntary associations, in maintaining membership and independence. He explains, "In defending her own freedom, the Church is also defending the human person ... [and] the various social organizations and nations—all of which enjoy their own spheres of autonomy and sovereignty" (*CA*, no. 45).

The contribution of CST in dealing with civil society is often dismissed *a priori* because it explicitly refers both to natural law and the concept of the common good. Its social teaching is based on a vision in which "the social nature of man is not completely fulfilled in the State, but is realized in various intermediary groups, beginning with the family and including economic, social, political and cultural groups which stem from human nature itself and have their own autonomy, always with a view to the common good" (*CA*, no. 13). At its core, CST is an understanding of human nature and the human condition.

Unfortunately, all too frequently, natural law concepts are used to justify policies based on an individual's particular definition of the common good. Acknowledging these misgivings, we believe that CST, especially as presented in *Gaudium et Spes* (*GS*) and the papal encyclicals *Centesimus Annus* (*CA*) and *Mater et Magistra* (*MM*), significantly contribute to understanding civil society.[1]

The focus of CST is to argue persuasively for individual freedom and participation in voluntary organizations. It is not to define policy for any particular society. We, therefore, take John Paul II seriously when he says that after careful study of current events, he does not intend CST to pass definitive judgment on policies (*CA*, no. 3). He further clarifies that the Church does

---

[1] Pope John XXIII, Encyclical Letter *Mater et Magistra* (1961), hereafter MM.

not attempt to present any overall model of socioeconomic life (*CA*, no. 43).

Collective terms such as "common good" and "national interest" are stumbling blocks for many; therefore, we wish to emphasize the concept of *positive externalities*, another term borrowed from economics. The term *positive externalities* describes benefits accruing to all from the stock of social capital. A positive externality, for example, is the benefit—financial or aesthetic—received by everyone in a neighborhood when one neighbor improves or maintains his or her property. Similarly, positive externalities result when individuals in a community act honestly and honor contracts.

As indicated, CST is based on the concept of natural law, interpreting it specifically as the means through which an individual becomes aware of his or her earthly and transcendent dignity. Thus, a denial of natural law deprives the person of standing and consequently leads to reorganization of society without reference to a person's dignity and responsibility (*CA*, no. 13). Class struggle, partisan interests, and ideology shape this reorganization in a way that is inconsistent with personal development. Those struggling with the concept of natural law, but who fear social chaos, must at least recognize the point at which contempt for the human person begins to place government-mandated social control above that of reason and law (*CA*, no. 14).

Embedding Social Capital

Social *capital* should in no way be confused with social *control*. Social capital refers to capabilities embodied in individuals and employed *by choice or habit* to benefit society as a whole. In this sense, social capital is a subset of human capital, not merely an amorphous substance floating around in the atmosphere of certain communities. Conventional human capital—education and skills—can be acquired independently from cooperative skills. However, to maintain the present stock of social capital, groups of individuals must choose to participate and accept the norms, disciplines, and objectives of particular autonomous organizations.

Technological know-how is embedded in capital equipment, such as computers, but also in individuals who have learned how to use the equipment. Similarly, formal organizations matter in the social sphere. Social capital is embedded both in people and within organizations.

Given the importance of organizations to the social sphere, the Northeast Regional Center for Rural Development at Pennsylvania State University publishes a Social Capital Index for every county in the United States. This Social Capital Index classifies each establishment in a specific county as being religious, civic, business, political, professional, labor, or recreational. The total number of organizations is then divided by populations and aggregated with three other variables: voter turnout, the census response rate, and the number of not-for-profit organizations.[2]

The Penn State Social Capital Index average for all US counties is approximately zero, because the primary use of this index is for regional comparisons. For example, the average 2014 index value for all counties in Indiana is negative 0.41, with a high of 0.78 for Jennings County and a low of negative 1.47 for Crawford County. The number of organizations per capita in Indiana (1.40) exceeds the national average (1.38). Also, Indiana counties show a higher response average to the 2010 Census (79%) versus US counties as a whole (70%). However, Indiana's overall Penn State Social Capital Index value is calculated as less than the average due to a lower voting rate in 2014 (58%) versus US counties as a whole (67%).

---

[2] Anil Rupasingha, Stephen J. Goetz, and David Freshwater, "The Production of Social Capital in US Counties," *Journal of Socio-Economics*, 35, no. 1 (2006): 83–101.

The goal of the Social Capital Index, therefore, is to indicate the existing number of organizations per capita and the prevalence of certain forms of civic behavior. While the Index is useful, it fails to capture an essential input of social capital formation that we wish to consider. Social capital is embodied both in organizations *and in people*; together they institutionalize cultural norms reflecting the priorities of a particular society.

The link between the social nature of persons and personal development within social institutions is addressed in *Gaudium et Spes*, the Second Vatican *Council's Pastoral Constitution on the Church in the Modern World*. A person's social life is not something added on but is essential to being human. An individual's destiny hinges on personal gifts developed through dealings and dialogue with others. Certain social ties, like family and nationality, are given, but others originate from free decision. In our times, mutual dependencies have given rise to a variety of associations and organizations, both public and private. This socialization, while certainly not without its dangers, brings with it many advantages with respect to consolidating and increasing the qualities of the human person (*GS*, no. 25).

The Great Decline in Social Capital

Charles Murray identifies the symptoms of what he, drawing on others such as Francis Fukuyama, refers to as the Great Disruption in social capital in the United States. These include increases in adolescent suicide and homicide, drug use, and incarceration; decreased attachment to employment; decaying neighborhoods; declining academic performance; reduced social mobility; increased out-of-wedlock births; and family breakdown.[3] Murray does not suggest that these are recent problems easily eliminated with optimal policy and resources. Sociologists, economists,

---

[3] Charles Murray, *Coming Apart: The State of White America, 1960–2010* (New York: Crown, 2012).

policy makers, and educators warn, however, that an upward trend in these indicators is a serious threat to democracy and presents obstacles to human development, particularly for the most vulnerable.

In the 1950s and early 1960s, family cohesion in the United States and Western Europe improved, as did fertility rates; therefore, any disruptions in social patterns, particularly increases in homicide and divorce rates, were late in being recognized. As the incidence of divorce, single-parent families, and out-of-wedlock births increased, the policy definition of family was stretched to include virtually any type of household, whether or not it included a mother, a father, and their biological children. Referring to the widespread acceptance of the decline in ordinary indicators of social wellbeing, the late Senator Daniel Patrick Moynihan coined the phrase "defining deviancy down."

Civil authorities and society, in general, have traditionally acknowledged the true nature of marriage and family. Of course, it is presumed that whenever families are incapable of assuming full responsibility for the young, the old, the sick, and the disabled, "other social bodies have the duty of helping them."[4] Nevertheless, regardless of circumstances, the family unit was seen as primary. Unfortunately, any acknowledgment of the primary tight bonds between fathers, mothers, and children has increasingly been overshadowed by the belief that government, community, and income transfers can substitute for kinship. However, it is becoming more difficult to ignore that children are anywhere from ten to over one hundred times more likely to suffer abuse at the hands of substitutes rather than natural parents.[5]

---

[4] *Catechism of the Catholic Church* (Vatican City: Libereria Editrice, 1994), no. 2209.

[5] Francis Fukuyama, "Social Capital," *The Tanner Lectures on Human Values*, Brasenose College, Oxford, UK, 1997, 408, https://tannerlectures.utah.edu/_documents/a-to-z/f/Fukuyama98.pdf.

Voluntary associations support rather than usurp the primary role of the family. However, a social function across virtually all human cultures, particularly when paternal authority is lacking, is the need to control the aggression of young males. Male initiation ceremonies that occur in tribal, fraternal, and military organizations are just one of the means through which older males socialize younger ones into the rules of their respective societies.[6] Less recognized is the need for young women to be mentored in managing a household, an undervalued skill. Such mentoring, for both young men and young women, is at risk, given declining participation in voluntary organizations.

Over-reliance on formal education for social formation does a disservice to both social capital and education. The decline in educational achievement of American primary and secondary students over the past two generations is well documented. There are many causes for this decline. However, the Coleman Report of the 1960s indicated that the single factor most reliably correlated with educational achievement is not per capita spending on education, standards, curriculum, computers in the classroom, teacher training, vouchers, or any of the other panaceas offered up as public policy solutions, but rather parents' involvement in their children's education.[7] Parents, in general, remain concerned about their inability to direct their children toward academic proficiency, careers, and the good life. This problem is aggravated by social isolation, by underestimating parents' adequacy versus that of professionals, and by the availability of fewer options for parents to be meaningfully involved in deciding what is best for their children. Before the consolidation of school districts, local public and parochial schools functioned much like cooperatives, with active and effective parental involvement.

---

[6] Fukuyama, "Social Capital," 408.
[7] Fukuyama, "Social Capital," 410.

One option for increasing parental involvement in children's education is (parental) school choice. Surprisingly, even with the increased availability of vouchers, enrollment in private elementary schools continues to decline. In 1958, the number of school-aged American children attending a private elementary school reached 15 percent. In the mid-1970s, the number had fallen to 10 percent, and in 2015, 9 percent.[8] Private elementary school enrollment rates indicate that this decline is not a low-income phenomenon. From 1968 to 2013, the proportion of children from middle-income families enrolled in private elementary schools declined by almost half. The exclusion of middle-income families from parochial schools is both a church and societal problem, related to means-tested eligibility for vouchers and other forms of financial aid.

Although our emphasis is on participation in private and quasi-private institutions, we do not attribute declining social capital to public schools in particular or as affecting only low-income sectors in the United States. Public school extracurricular activities play a critical role in social capital formation, and many low-income families have been able to avoid social disruption. Poverty and inadequate educational opportunities certainly are factors in declining social capital, but causality does not necessarily go from low-income families to pathological social breakdown.

It is possible, of course, to identify a syndrome characterizing low-income households and social dysfunction. Murray's research

---

[8] Richard J. Murnane et al., "Who Goes to Private School?" *Education Next* 18, no. 4 (Fall 2018), https://www.educationnext.org/who-goes-private-school-long-term-enrollment-trends-family-income/. Two previous volumes in this series have explored this and related educational issues: Kevin E. Schmiesing, *Catholic Education and the Promise of School Choice* (Grand Rapids: Acton Institute, 2012); and Christiaan Alting von Geusau and Phillip Booth, *Catholic Education in the West: Roots, Reality, and Revival* (Grand Rapids: Acton Institute, 2013).

clearly describes how households living in affluent districts are more likely to be able to immunize themselves from the Great Disruption. Our objective is to suggest that increasing social interactions may be an effective, low-cost option for creating social capital. By the mid-nineties, it became obvious that income transfers and public funds for education from pre-K through graduate school are not the solution to declining social capital.

Murray's concluding insight is simple but powerful: There is a need for those who consider themselves social democrats to be honest in explaining how affluent families protect themselves from social dysfunction by adopting certain behaviors.[9] It might be better yet to increase opportunities in the public square so that all households, regardless of income, discover and learn how to acquire social capital and avoid dysfunctional behaviors.

---

[9] Murray, *Coming Apart*, 300.

III Opportunities to Practice and Gain Social Capital

The state can make the exercise of freedom more difficult or less difficult, but it cannot destroy personal initiative. "Not only is it wrong from the ethical point of view to disregard human nature, which is made for freedom, but in practice, it is impossible to do so. Where society is so organized as to reduce arbitrarily or even suppress the sphere in which freedom is legitimately exercised, the result is that the life of society becomes progressively disorganized and goes into decline" (*CA*, no. 25).

John Paul II makes it abundantly clear how a person's effectiveness is naturally interrelated with the work of others. Goods and services in our times, he writes, cannot be created through the work of an isolated individual; they require the cooperation of many people working toward a common goal. Man's intelligence, discipline, and close cooperation with others enable him to discover the earth's potential. "Important virtues are involved in this process, such as diligence, industriousness, prudence in undertaking reasonable risks, reliability and fidelity in interpersonal relationships, as well as courage in carrying out decisions which are difficult and painful but necessary, both for the overall working of a business and in meeting possible set-backs" (*CA*, no. 32).

Concerning the production function for goods and services, economists quantify how many hours of labor and how much invested capital/machinery it takes to deliver, for example, one hundred hamburgers at McDonald's. There are lively discussions at conferences about where the technology to grow national output is embedded: Is value created by the equipment or is value created by the person using the equipment? Or, is value creation due to disembodied, increased knowledge? Social philosophers believe that societal wellbeing is a function not just of families and institutions but also of prevailing social norms. These social norms reflect priorities and whatever it is that a particular culture values. The question to be explored is: How are social norms that are required for effective organizations inculcated in individuals?

In the United States, an individual's credit score is a measurement used to determine a person's estimated creditworthiness (the probability that he or she will repay a debt). The credit score allows financial institutions to evaluate the risk of a client becoming insolvent. A similar score is being developed in China, but it is much more encompassing and has more to do with social control than social capital. Beijing is working on a "social credit" system scheduled to become obligatory starting in 2020. The State Council is creating an extensive database covering a wide range of activities of individual citizens. This database will allow authorities to evaluate "trustworthiness" of individuals and to discriminate between individuals who are more or less "virtuous."[1] Such an intrusive and arbitrary measure, even in the face of declining social capital, is not an acceptable option in the United States. What may be required in a democratic free-enterprise system is a large number of residents *voluntarily* choosing to act in ways that maintain or increase existing social capital.

---

[1] Paul De Maeyer, "The Chinese 'Social Credit System': The Real Big Brother of the Future?" *Aleteia*, June 28, 2018, https://aleteia.org/2018/06/28/the-chinese-social-credit-system-the-real-big-brother-of-the-future/.

Philosopher Alasdair MacIntyre refers to virtues as those traits necessary for first imagining and then cultivating better communities. Individuals cannot grow from totally dependent infants to relative independence without exercising certain virtues, and the means for practicing virtue requires sustained assistance from others. The sociopolitical community exists, according to MacIntyre, to foster cooperative reasoning about common goals. Through such engagement, an individual rationally comes to terms with his or her aspirations and limitations. Communities smaller than the nation-state and significantly smaller than global organizations are the public spaces through which a genuine common good is debated and nourished.

MacIntyre argues that, to assume and sustain one's role in society, individuals need opportunities to practice virtue. It is this "practice" we wish to emphasize. He defines practice as any form of cooperative human activity through which desirable outcomes result as individuals acquire skills needed to achieve excellence. He recognizes that these outcomes may result in prizes, prestige, status, or income, but he focuses on the internal qualities, including virtue, acquired by those participating in these activities. A practice involves standards of excellence and obedience to rules, and this eliminates self-judging one's performance. MacIntyre states that outcomes derived from individuals striving and cooperating to achieve excellence in art, athletics, homemaking, farming, governance, and so on benefit the whole community.[2]

For MacIntyre, the pursuit of virtue emphasizes human interdependence and the common good. As free-market economists, we are aware that MacIntyre's approach deemphasizes competition pitting the individual against the group, whereas economists tend to emphasize the importance of competing

---

[2] Alasdair MacIntyre, *After Virtue: A Study in Moral Theory*, 2nd ed. (Notre Dame: University of Notre Dame Press, 1984), 187–91.

institutions. We agree, however, on the need for associations to remediate deficiencies and that, through close association with other individuals, each person attains a degree of perfection in line with his or her intensely social nature. The more intense the association, the greater the development.[3]

Certain thinkers express reservations with MacIntyre's approach. It is not because they minimize the positive effects of virtuous behavior. They suggest rather that a more realistic approach would be a return to a liberal order based on the ideas of the Enlightenment. To simplify, this liberal agenda ("liberal" in the eighteenth-century use of the word) is one based on formal social contracts among rational individuals.

Others critique MacIntyre's emphasis on personal growth rather than acquiring virtue for the sake of one's eternal destiny. For example, Gilbert Meilaender argues against sublimating one's particular goals and responsibilities for an undefined common good. Although we define the public good in terms of realized positive externalities, our focus is on describing an environment that facilitates personal fulfillment through group participation. Catholic social thought recognizes the role of private organizations in achieving this earthly social objective.[4] Meilaender, as well, expresses support for a community with vibrant organizations in the public square trying to reconcile conflicting interests.[5]

There appears to be a consensus that social capital formation requires freedom for a large number of intermediaries in the

---

[3] Charles M. Horvath, "Excellence versus Effectiveness: MacIntyre's Critique of Business," *Business Ethics Quarterly* 5, no. 3 (July 1995): 499–532.

[4] *Catechism of the Catholic Church*, nos. 1906–1910.

[5] Gilbert Meilaender, Review of Alasdair MacIntyre, *Dependent Rational Animals: Why Human Beings Need the Virtues* (Open Court, 1999) and the *MacIntyre Reader*, Kelvin Knight, ed. (University of Notre Dame Press, 1998), *First Things*, October 1999.

public square with a high degree of participation. As part of their given role within a particular organization, persons engage in a value-revealing process. Here, they gain the ability to assess and judge their own and others' performance. When these opportunities to practice cooperative skills are restricted, the stock of social capital declines. A lack of interpersonal engagement corrupts formal and informal institutions based on embodied values and traditions.[6]

What specific norms or virtues foster working together effectively? Western economic development gives priority to truth-telling, the meeting of obligations, and reciprocity. There is, however, some discussion on whether or not these values deemphasize cooperative behavior. The disruption of families, localities, and loyalties is often interpreted as a result of tolerance for self-interested behavior. However, personal freedom and a certain degree of leisure, generated through free enterprise, are necessary for the formation of private organizations. Our intent here is not to explore the differences between collective versus commercial activity but rather to stress the importance of nongovernment organizations' contribution to social capital.[7]

Catholic social teaching is based on a vision in which "the social nature of man is not completely fulfilled in the State. Alternatively, it is also realized in various intermediary groups, beginning with the family but also including economic, social, political and cultural groups which stem from human nature itself and have their own autonomy, always with a view to the common good" (*CA*, no. 13). In any society, the priority given certain norms varies, and the trade-offs between economic and social goals are recognized. Nevertheless, it is difficult to imagine

---

[6] MacIntyre, *After Virtue*, 223.

[7] For an extended discussion of differences between types of organizations see Barry P. Keating and Maryann O. Keating, *Microeconomics for Public Managers* (Chichester, UK: Wiley-Blackwell, 2009).

an inherent contradiction between virtues that enable individuals to cooperate effectively in government and those that enable them to do so in the market or through social intermediaries.

Trust and Collective Action

In his Tanner Lectures at Oxford University, Francis Fukuyama, an American political scientist and economist, addressed declining social capital taking place over three decades from 1965 through 1995. Fukuyama described how game theory literature and simulations study the emergence of spontaneously generated informal norms regulating behavior. Simulations of people interacting with one another lend support to the assumption, not fully accepted by Fukuyama, that norms arise spontaneously out of self-interested interactions.[8]

Fukuyama analyzes the concept of spontaneous social capital creation in the economics literature. The Nobel-winning economist Ronald Coase believed that the self-interested interactions of individuals do not need to be mandated through law or formal institutions. People negatively impacted by the behavior of others have a rational incentive to organize and buy off those offending them. Similarly, with English common law in mind, Friedrich Hayek also argued that social norms are generally not legislated through a formal political process but are rather the result of the repeated interactions of individuals seeking to achieve common aims.[9]

Fukuyama takes a step further and concludes that social cooperation may be hard-wired into the genetic structure of humans. Thus, through repeated interactions with one another, people may be able to achieve a state of satisfactory cooperation. However, Fukuyama concludes that there may be strong

---

[8] Fukuyama, "Social Capital," 465.
[9] F. A. Hayek, *The Road to Serfdom* (1944, repr. Chicago: University of Chicago Press, 2007).

cultural and biological impulses toward cooperative behavior but questions why it is that cooperation often breaks down.

Human beings, according to Fukujama, have a natural tendency both to cooperate and to disrupt. Historically, norms were transmitted to subsequent generations through a complex process of socialization, ranging from family to formal education. In the modern world, ideas cross political and cultural borders more rapidly and become a basis for group affiliation. Increasing exposure to global media and use of online social media networks take much less effort than participating in formal organizations and may facilitate adaptation to newer (and somewhat different) norms of behavior within a short period.

Social capital, as we define it, is a stock inculcated through practice; whereas Fukuyama's network of trust accrues to society at large, as a type of positive externality rather than any intentional collective practice. Local cooperation, either desirable or undesirable, depends on values widely held and practiced by a large percentage of a population. However, according to Fukuyama, a functioning civic society is characterized by a certain level of trust conducive to nonfamily collective decision-making.[10]

During the early postwar period, two changes contributed to decreased socialization and networks of trust. The first change involved medical technology (i.e., birth control and easy access to abortion), and the second change was the ease of movement of women into the paid labor force with earnings that increased their earned incomes relative to men.

The significance of birth control was not that it lowered fertility, since fertility had been on the decline in many societies before the widespread availability of birth control.[11] Indeed, if the effect of birth control is to reduce the number of unwanted

---

[10] Fukuyama, "Social Capital," 428–31

[11] Fukuyama, "Social Capital," 418.

pregnancies, it is difficult to explain why it accompanied a rise in the rate of abortions or why the use of birth control is positively correlated with out-of-wedlock births across the most economically advanced countries. The main impact of the sexual revolution appears to have been that it lowered the perceived risk in sexual relations and dramatically changed male behavior. This growth in male irresponsibility reinforced the female drive for independence and reduced the incidence of two-parent families.

Fukuyama is pessimistic about whether we are moving spontaneously towards generally accepted new norms to substitute for traditional norms that were responsible for the optimal socialization of children. He concludes that declining levels of social capital in the United States are essentially a result of the extent to which Western societies prize individualism and denigrate the importance of virtually all inherited social duties and obligations.[12]

On a more positive note, Fukuyama suggests that one of the most important sources of social capital in a postindustrial economy is professional education. It is through a learning process that engineers, doctors, lawyers, accountants, and architects not only are trained in their particular field of specialty but also are socialized to obey certain behavioral norms concerning professional standards. This supports our focus on intermediary institutions. Opportunities for acquiring social capital should not be reserved for a professional elite but rather practiced on the assembly lines and in bowling leagues, by plumbers and nuclear scientists alike.

---

[12] Fukuyama, "Social Capital," 401–5.

IV Declines in Voluntary, Civic, and Religious Participation

Marxism affirms that alienation can only be eliminated in a collective society, but experience shows that collectivism increases alienation. Unfortunately, the loss of the authentic meaning of life is a reality in Western societies as well. Alienation occurs, according to John Paul II, when persons do not have a genuinely supportive community and thus experience increased isolation within a maze of relationships marked by destructive competitiveness and estrangement (*CA*, no. 41).

The Dropout Cohort

Robert Putnam, like Fukuyama, has written extensively on the erosion of social capital. However, Putnam focuses on organizations and declining participation in those organizations. At all levels of education and among both men and women, the United States experienced a drop of roughly one-quarter in group membership from 1974 to the mid-nineties, about the time Putnam's book *Bowling Alone* was published. Membership decline affected all types of groups, from sports clubs to professional associations, from discussion groups to labor unions. Church attendance in the United States fell by 15 percent during the 1960s, and by the mid-nineties, regular attendance consisted of roughly only 30 percent of the total population.[1]

Putnam identified declining American participation in organizations as an important factor in the erosion of social capital but was unable to pinpoint the cause of this decline. Particularly frustrating to him was that, contrary to evidence suggesting that education boosts civic awareness, educational levels rose as participation fell throughout the period studied. Therefore, Putnam proceeds, like a detective in a mystery novel, to list and evaluate factors potentially associated with this decline; the list of suspects is presented in table 1.

Table I
Possible Explanations for the Erosion of Social Capital

- Time Pressure
- Economic Hard Times
- Residential Mobility
- Suburbanization
- Movement of Women into the Labor Force
- Disruption of Marriage and Family Ties
- Changes in Structure of the American Economy
- Disillusion with Government and the Cultural Revolution
- The Growth of the Welfare State
- The Civil Rights Movement
- Television, Electronics, and Other Technological Change

One by one, Putnam eliminated factors in table 1 as important in explaining the decline in participation. Rates of residential mobility were remarkably constant over the period studied.

---

[1] Robert D. Putnam, "Tuning In, Tuning Out: The Strange Disappearance of Social Capital in America," *Political Science and Politics* 28, no. 4 (December 1995): 664–83.

Evidence strongly suggests that long hours on the job are not associated with less involvement in civic life. Also, declines in engagement are somewhat greater among the affluent segments of the American public.[2] Putnam, however, was inclined to dismiss the effect of big government and the welfare state, points with which we will take exception later.

Putnam found that rates of association do not differ greatly between large cities, suburbs, smaller cities, and rural areas. Furthermore, he dismissed the hypothesis that whites withdrew from community organizations during the Civil Rights era; racial differences in declining membership are not significant and the erosion in participation affected all races. Membership decline was essentially identical among whites who favored segregation, whites who opposed it, and blacks in general.[3]

Although the absolute declines in joining are approximately equivalent among men and women, Putnam found the relative declines to be somewhat greater for women. Surprisingly, women working outside the home participate slightly more in voluntary organizations than women in general. Divorce, per Putnam, was not a major cause of the membership decline, but divorce itself may be a consequence, not the cause, of lower social capital. Controlling for education, age, race, and so on, single people—both men and women, divorced, separated, and never-married—were significantly less trusting and less engaged in civic organizations than married people.[4]

Putnam found that the notable exception to the uniformity of the decline in social participation is age. Older people, in his research, participated more in formal organizations than young people. Older American also voted at a higher rate, read newspapers more frequently, and engaged in more civic activities.

---

[2] Putnam, "Tuning In, Tuning Out," 669.

[3] Putnam, "Tuning In, Tuning Out," 673.

[4] Putnam, "Tuning In, Tuning Out," 670–71.

At first, Putnam was inclined to attribute the correlation between participation and age to a life-cycle pattern. However, between 1972 and 1994, as various generations moved through time, membership levels more often fell than rose. He wondered if this could be a "period effect," a sign of the times. However, he concluded that a "generational effect" offers a better explanation. Successive generations with divergent outlooks enter and leave the populations, and each generation has a certain propensity to participate.

Cohort analysis, Putnam concluded, explained the generational effect, but unfortunately, it did not answer the question of why generations differ on their propensity to participate.[5] However, pinpointing the cohort and the decade in which a particular generation was young do offer clues. Men and women born in the late 1920s and early 1930s joined, trusted, voted, and read newspapers at a rate higher than other cohorts over a forty-year period. Controlling for educational disparities, members of this generation were twice as likely to belong to civic associations as those born in the late 1960s.

Putnam asked why it took researchers so long to recognize this generational effect. It was not until the 1960s, 1970s, and 1980s that the decline in attendance and volunteer lists for PTA meetings, Masonic lodges, Red Cross, Boy Scouts, polling stations, and churches became conspicuous. As the older, attached generation hit their stride and became dominant, the "post-civic" cohort participated less.

Could increases in divorce and percentages of mothers working away from home explain the decline? These factors peaked only after childhood for Putnam's "post-civic" cohort, growing up in the fifties. The introduction and dominance of television viewing is the single factor Putnam found to be consistent with the timing of this generation. It appears that newspaper read-

---

[5] Putnam, "Tuning In, Tuning Out," 674).

ing is associated with high social capital and TV viewing with low social capital.

We, therefore, detect a soft technological determinism in Putnam's conclusion, in which he attributed a fragmenting effect on society and culture to changes in communication technology.[6] Although Putnam and Fukuyama differ in methodology, Putnam's conclusion is quite similar to Fukuyama's in that both emphasize the importance of technological changes. Fukuyama attributes massive shifts in norms and values to the media, as well as to global trends and travel.

Will social platforms such as Facebook, LinkedIn, Twitter, and Instagram have a profound effect on social capital accumulation for the present generation? Will the effect be positive or negative? At this point, it is premature to speculate whether, on net, social media is reversing or contributing to the negative trend in social capital, the ability to work together to achieve a common objective.

Much of the debate over Putnam's research concerns his use of organizational attachment to assess an across-the-board decline in social capital over two generations. Critics suggest that the distribution of social capital among socioeconomic groups may be more significant than an overall decline. We, however, support Putnam's emphasis on organizational participation as the effective means for accumulating social capital. Using a computer analogy, social capital, embodied in persons (users), is acquired when practiced within organizations (hardware). In the next section, we try to determine whether Putnam's declining participation effect extends into the first two decades of the twenty-first century.

---

[6] Putnam, "Tuning In, Tuning Out," 680.

Choosing How to Allocate Time

Given the abundance of data, it may seem obvious that changes in social capital could be assessed by measuring rates of homicide, assault, rape, burglary, suicide, and addiction. The problem is that social deviance ignores distribution and, therefore, any overall net change in social capital. That is, a high incidence of social capital, widely distributed across the United States, might coexist with pockets of extreme social pathology that drive up rates of homicide, assault, and so forth. A more accurate indicator of changes in the overall stock of social capital, therefore, may be statistics concerning how people voluntarily choose to allocate their time.

The *American Time Use Survey* (*ATUS*) measures the amount of time people, throughout the country, spend doing various activities, such as paid work, childcare, volunteering, and socializing. The *ATUS* data are collected via telephone interviews. Respondents receive an advance letter and pamphlet explaining the purpose of the *ATUS* and notifying them of the day they will be called. The *ATUS* interview is based on a twenty-four-hour time diary, starting at 4:00 a.m. the previous day and ending at 4:00 a.m. on the interview day. Participation percentages for activities relevant to our study are presented in table 2. They represent annual averages on any given day of the week for the civilian noninstitutional population, ages fifteen and over.

Table 2 lends support to Putnam's work through the mid-1990s on declining social capital, defined here as potential benefits created when people exercise their ability to voluntarily work together to achieve common objectives. From 2003 through 2017, Americans, both men and women, reduced their participation in voluntary and civic activities. For most activities, the trend line over the period was negative and statistically significant. There is some indication that men on average increased their participation in cultural and women in social service activities, but these trends are not statistically significant.

What is particularly interesting is the positive and significant trend in all religious and spiritual activities. Note, however, that this is associated with a negative trend in actual time spent in attending formal religious services. The data presented in table 2 is the average across all days of the week. Of particular interest is the statistically significant negative trend for both men and women in attending formal religious services. At the time the survey was taken, the personal value of participation in organized activities, including attendance at religious services, was continuing to decline.

If Americans are traveling less to participate in organized activities, what are they doing with their time? Are they spending more time caring for and assisting adult household and nonhousehold members? Indeed, the percentage of men caring for household adults is increasing and statistically significant, but at 2 percent in 2017 represents a minuscule percentage. On the other hand, 8.1 percent of American women and 6.3 percent of American men on an average day report caring for and helping nonhousehold adults. Overall, however, the trend in the actual amount of time spent daily in caring for nonhousehold adults is negative and significant both for both men and women. In sum, the *American Time Use Survey*, table 2, on pages 28–30 confirms a persistent decline in activities we believe to be associated with the formation of social capital.

Table 2

The *American Time Use Survey* (*ATUS*) of Adult American Participation in Religious, Civic, and Volunteer Activities and in Caring for Other Adults

ACTIVITY	Percent Participating on an Average Day—Age 15 Years and Above		*P value = 0.05 or less
	Year 2017	Slope of the Linerar Trend Line 2003–2014	Slope Statistically Significant*
Religious and spiritual activities	9.3	positive	yes
Religious and spiritual activities, Men	6.8	positive	yes
Religious and spiritual activities, Women	11.7	positive	yes
Attending religious services	4.1	negative	yes
Attending religious services, Men	3.5	negative	yes
Attending religious services, Women	4.7	negative	yes
Participation in religious practices	5.5	positive	yes
Participation in religious practices, Men	3.6	positive	yes
Participation in religious practices, Women	7.2	positive	yes
Volunteering (organizational and civic activities)	6.1	negative	yes
Volunteering (organizational and civic activities), Men	4.5	negative	yes
Volunteering (organizational and civic activities), Women	7.6	negative	yes
Volunteer activities	6.0	negative	yes
Volunteer activities, Men	4.4	negative	yes
Volunteer activities, Women	7.4	negative	no
Administrative and support activities (volunteering)	2.3	negative	no
Administrative and support activities (volunteering), Men	1.4	negative	no
Administrative and support activities (volunteering), Women	3.1	negative	no

Declines in Voluntary, Civic, and Religious Participation

Percent Participating on an Average Day—Age 15 Years and Above			*P value = 0.05 or less
ACTIVITY	Year 2017	Slope of the Linerar Trend Line 2003–2014	Slope Statistically Significant*
Social service and care activities (volunteering)	1.8	negative	no
Social service and care activities (volunteering), Men	1.2	negative	yes
Social service and care activities (volunteering), Women	2.5	positive	no
Indoor and outdoor maintenance, building, and cleanup activities (volunteering)	0.4	negative	no
Indoor and outdoor maintenance, building, and cleanup activities (volunteering), Men	0.4	negative	yes
Indoor and outdoor maintenance, building, and cleanup activities (volunteering), Women	0.3	negative	no
Participating in performance and cultural activities (volunteering)	0.5	0	no
Participating in performance and cultural activities (volunteering), Men	0.5	positive	no
Participating in performance and cultural activities (volunteering), Women	0.5	negative	no
Attending meetings, conferences, and training (volunteering)	0.7	negative	no
Attending meetings, conferences, and training (volunteering), Men	0.5	negative	no
Attending meetings, conferences, and training (volunteering), Women	0.9	0	no
Civic obligations and participation	0.1	0	no
Civic obligations and participation, Men	0.1	0	no
Civic obligations and participation, Women	0.2	positive	no

Percent Participating on an Average Day—Age 15 Years and Above			*P value = 0.05 or less
ACTIVITY	Year 2017	Slope of the Linerar Trend Line 2003–2014	Slope Statistically Significant*
Travel related to organizational, civic, and religious activities	7.6	negative	yes
Travel related to organizational, civic, and religious activities, Men	6.3	negative	yes
Travel related to organizational, civic, and religious activities, Women	8.8	negative	yes
Caring for and helping household adults	6.0	positive	no
Caring for and helping household adults, Men	5.5	negative	no
Caring for and helping household adults, Women	6.5	positive	no
Caring for household adults	2.5	positive	no
Caring for household adults, Men	2.0	positive	yes
Caring for household adults, Women	2.9	positive	no
Physical care for household adults	1.7	positive	yes
Physical care for household adults, Men	1.5	positive	no
Physical care for household adults, Women	1.8	positive	no
Helping household adults	4.0	negative	no
Helping household adults, Men	3.8	negative	yes
Helping household adults, Women	4.3	negative	no
Caring for and helping nonhousehold adults	7.2	negative	yes
Caring for and helping nonhousehold adults, Men	6.3	negative	yes
Caring for and helping nonhousehold adults, Women	8.1	negative	yes
Caring for nonhousehold adults	0.7	negative	no
Caring for nonhousehold adults, Men	0.5	negative	yes
Caring for nonhousehold adults, Women	1.0	negative	yes
Helping nonhousehold adults	6.9	negative	no
Helping nonhousehold adults, Men	6.1	negative	no
Helping nonhousehold adults, Women	7.6	negative	yes

Source of Data: United States Department of Labor. Bureau of Labor Statistics, https://www.bls.gov/tus/atusfaqs.htm#4.

Youth: Engaged and Disengaged

The United States is often characterized as a youth-oriented society. Is it the case then that social capital accumulation in the United States is focused primarily on teenagers?

The Stanford Inter-university Consortium for Political and Social Research in 2011–2013 conducted a civic participation study of 1,578 California high school seniors. Participating schools were selected based on ethnic, socioeconomic, and immigrant diversity; these schools represent three different California regions. Seniors, as a part of the study, were invited during a required class period to participate in the survey. Of 1,678 students surveyed, approximately 84 percent were born in the United States and 52 percent were female.[7]

The Stanford Civic Purpose Study focused primarily on civic/political engagement. There is a subtle difference, not necessarily exclusive, between civic participation—how a resident or citizen relates to a particular political entity—and our focus on civil society—how individuals relate to one another in all types of voluntary organizations. Nevertheless, the Civic Purpose Project data is valuable, first in understanding youthful attitudes on participation and, secondly, in ranking students most likely to participate in organized athletic, ethnic, academic, volunteer, and religious activities.

Survey students were asked to select up to three, if any, of the issues, listed in table 3, about which they were most concerned. Given an open response opportunity, students reported concerns about gangs, drugs, personal safety, family, child abuse, and animal rights.

---

[7] William Damon, *Standard Civic Purpose Project: Longitudinal Study of Youth Civic Engagement in California, 2011–2013* (Ann Arbor, MI: Inter-university Consortium for Political and Social Research, 2017).

As expected, high school seniors in table 3 rank personal issues such as jobs, college, and the economy, of greater concern than world poverty, war, and the environment. If the goal is to increase social capital, youth groups would focus on personal development, not politicization. Agencies would do well to respect and relate to youthful aspirations as expressed rather than channeling student energies exclusively toward the goals of organizers.

Table 3

Social and Political Issues Identified by California High School Seniors as Those of Most Personal Concern

Social and Political Issues of Concern	Percentage Listing These Issues as One of Three of Most Concern
Availability of good jobs	35.1
Access to affordable college	32.1
The U.S. economy	23.1
Immigrant rights	23.1
Homelessness in my community	22.3
Discrimination and prejudice against minorities	19.7
The health care system	17.6
The environment	15.6
Drug and alcohol abuse	14.8
Teen pregnancy	14.1
Violence in my community	12.3
Gay and lesbian rights	12.1
Human rights throughout the world	10.9
Poverty in very poor countries	9.6
Failing schools in America	9.4
The war in Afghanistan	5.6
Women's rights	3.1

Source: Stanford Civic Purpose Project

To identify the characteristics of students fully engaged/disengaged in private nonpolitical activities, we employ a classification predictive analytics algorithm.

Classification algorithms are increasingly being used, not without criticism, to predict customer susceptibility to advertising, to project which prisoners will become repeat criminals, and to determine life expectancy. In this study, the classification technique is limited to a group of anonymous students self-reporting on personal characteristics. Our purpose is to determine whether these characteristics can be used to identify students most likely to be engaged/disengaged in organized activities, to participate in religious programs, and to volunteer.

Unlike regression analysis, a classification algorithm does not decide *a priori* that variables available in a database are likely to be most significant. The algorithm allows the data to build a model for selecting students most likely to participate in a particular activity if a pattern of participation is present in the data. In no way does identifying important attributes contributing to accurate classification imply causality or quantify the associational attachment of an individual student.

The object of classification is to rank survey respondents as either *engaged* or *not engaged* in a particular activity based on a set of shared characteristics. To do this, the data set is randomly divided into two groups of respondents. One group, referred to as the training data set, is used to build the classification model. Then, the accuracy of the model built on the characteristics/attributes of this first group attempts to classify the second group, referred to as the validation data set. The classification of students in the Stanford study as participating in various activities is presented in table 4 on pages 34–37.

Table 4. A Classification Model for Teens Presently Engaged in Various Activities

TARGETS	ENGAGED[1]	DISENGAGED[2]	REGULAR RELIGIOUS PARTICIPATION[3]	REGULAR OR SOME RELIGIOUS PARTICIPATION[4]	VOLUNTEER[5]
Percentage of Total Students Surveyed:	56.53%	9%	12.61%	26.68%	23.45%
Accuracy of Classification into Target Group:	Training 81.6% Testing 70.9%	Training 97.8% Testing 77.1%	Training 92.4% Testing 85.6%	Training 84.5% Testing 75.6%	Training 87.9% Testing 75.3%
Attributes Used to Classify:					
• Gender					
• Born in U.S.					
How Meaningful to You Are:					
• Having a high-paying job					
• Helping others in need				Important Predictor	Important Predictor
• Having my own family			Important Predictor		
• Devoting attention to my religious or spiritual life	Important Predictor		Important Predictor	Important Predictor	
• Good neighbors who care about me			Important Predictor		

Declines in Voluntary, Civic, and Religious Participation

• A school that cares about kids and encourages them					Important Predictor			
• Teachers who urge me to develop and achieve		Important Predictor			Important Predictor			
• Support from adults other than my parents.		Important Predictor						
Your Motivation to Participate:								
• It is required at school.								
• It makes me feel good about myself.								Important Predictor
• To further my education or career goals								Important Predictor
• Somebody asked or encouraged me to participate.						Important Predictor		
• To build skills or prepare for the future.		Important Predictor			Important Predictor			Important Predictor
• I wanted to be the kind of person who helps others.								Important Predictor
• It sounded fun.								
• It is important for my religious/ ethnic/cultural group.					Important Predictor	Important Predictor		

TARGETS	ENGAGED[1]	DISENGAGED[2]	REGULAR RELIGIOUS PARTICIPATION[3]	REGULAR OR SOME RELIGIOUS PARTICIPATION[4]	VOLUNTEER[5]
You Consider Yourself:					
• Spiritual or religious	Important Predictor		Important Predictor	Important Predictor	
• Smart	Important Predictor				
• Willing to stand up for what I believe is right					
• Creative or imaginative			Important Predictor	Important Predictor	
• Compassionate, concerned about all kinds of people	Important Predictor	Important Predictor			
• Honest					
• Concerned about government decisions and policies	Important Predictor	Important Predictor			
• Rebellious		Important Predictor			
• Responsible, someone others can depend on		Important Predictor			Important Predictor
• Outgoing		Important Predictor			Important Predictor
• Athletic	Important Predictor	Important Predictor	Important Predictor		

Declines in Voluntary, Civic, and Religious Participation

I am active in organizations or social groups that include mostly members of my own ethnic group.					Important Predictor
You often feel that you, personally, have been discriminated against for any reason?	Important Predictor	Important Predictor		Important Predictor	
It is important to my friends to go to parties.		Important Predictor			
It is important to my friends to get good grades.					Important Predictor
You Agree/Disagree:					
• My parents/guardians are active in the community.	Important Predictor				Important Predictor
• My parents/guardians do volunteer work in the community			Important Predictor	Important Predictor	
• I have a good sense of what makes my life meaningful					

Data Source: Stanford Civic Purpose Project: Longitudinal Study of Youth Civic Engagement in California, 2011–2013.

[1] **Engaged**—Those students indicating that since starting high school they have regularly participated in a religious, ethnic, political, arts, academic, or sports organization, team, or club.

[2] **Disengaged**—Those students indicating that since starting high school they have never participated in a religious, ethnic, political, arts, academic, or sports organization, team, or club.

[3] **Regular Religious Participation**—Those students indicating that since starting high school they have regularly participated with a religious group.

[4] **Regular or Some Religious Participation**—Those students indicating that since starting high school they have regularly or a few times participated with a religious group.

[5] **Volunteer**—Students indicating that they are very involved in volunteer activities.

Table 4 supports, for the most part, what we believed intuitively about engaged students. That is, such high school students tend to be idealistic, self-interested, have community support, and identify as being smart and athletic. Less obvious is that those who identify as being spiritual, are associated with an ethnic group, or have family members who volunteer, are themselves most likely to be in this category. The important point is that faith and ethnic identification are attributes that are significant contributors to predicting which high school students choose to be engaged.[8]

The *disengaged*—those who have never participated—represent 9 percent of the total. Note the high degree of accuracy (between 78 percent and 98 percent) with which the classification model identifies the disengaged. It is, therefore, useful to examine those attributes identified as important predictors of being disengaged.

---

[8] The standard measure of effectiveness for a classification model is the percentage accuracy with which it can identify respondents in the validation group that were not used to formulate the model. This model identified with approximately 75 percent accuracy that students would be engaged. Our classification model is significantly better than the naïve model based solely on the average percentage of students who are engaged.

Two additional pieces of information from the classification are important. The first is that the model ranks all respondents from those most likely to be engaged to those who are least likely. The naïve model suggests that the first 40 percent of random respondents would contain 40 percent or the average number of engaged. However, our classification model of ranked data correctly classified approximately 60 percent of those actually engaged into the first 40 percent of the scored data (i.e., reordered data). The second piece of valuable information, presented for the target engaged in table 4, is the identification, given survey data, of those attributes that contributed the most in ranking students.

The engaged and disengaged share important predictors, but each group differs significantly in how they responded to the questions. For example, the disengaged do not identify as being athletic while the engaged do. The disengaged neither feel supported by adults outside the family nor are they active in ethnic-type associations, whereas the engaged report being supported by nonfamily adults and tend to be active in ethnic associations. Also, the disengaged consider themselves more likely to have experienced discrimination and to be rebellious.

Separately, we used an ensemble classification model to target students who regularly and those who regularly or occasionally participate in religious organizations. In table 4, these two groups are defined respectively as regular religious participation and regular or some religious participation. From this ensemble model, two important considerations are relevant for those sponsoring religious activities for youths. First, students who identify as being religious and who express the goal of devoting attention to their spiritual lives and character are more likely to regularly participate in religious activities. This, of course, is obvious, but the critical point is that the desire to participate in religion originates in the person, not with the organizers. Marketing undergraduates studying Maslow's hierarchy of needs learn that organizations do not create needs but respond to them.

The second finding for the regular or some category supports our personal experience that being invited or encouraged is an important predictor for participation in any activity.[9]

About 24 percent of the students in the Stanford survey reported currently working for pay, a tried and true means for American youth to accumulate social capital. Because this data did not include economic variables, we were unable to classify,

---

[9] It is somewhat surprising to us that neither gender nor US birth show up as important predictors for any of these activities.

with a high degree of accuracy, students by characteristics related to active employment.

The relatively low level of participation for high school seniors in voluntary and work activities contrasts with 98 percent reportedly planning to enroll in either a two- or four-year college following graduation. Yet, the National Student Clearinghouse reports that six years after enrolling in college more than 30 percent of students have not completed their degrees or have dropped out completely.

What social institutions, aside from family and friends, are available to former students? For more than a century in the United States, we have depended on school-related extracurricular activities to diffuse among all income levels what we now call "soft skills": strong work habits, self-discipline, teamwork, leadership, and a sense of civic engagement. Putnam indicates that even in states such as California where pay-to-play policies in public schools are considered unconstitutional, the total cost of extracurricular participation might be four hundred dollars per activity per year.[10] Putnam laments that fostering opportunities for youth has become primarily a family rather than a community responsibility, such that youth from low-income households are now less likely to engage in extracurricular activities than previously.

---

[10] Putnam, *Our Kids*, 174.

V Linking Social Capital with Participation in Organizations

Levels of cooperation, participation, social interaction, and trust are characteristics that differentiate societies exhibiting various degrees of social capital. Civic and cooperative behavior is a cultural trait transmitted from generation to generation. Cultural traits in and of themselves are informal institutions interacting with formal institutions such as laws and regulations, which in turn affect organizational behavior.[1] The distinction between norms, institutions, and formal organizations assists in understanding the process whereby social capital is formed.

Formal organizations are relevant to the discussion of rebuilding social capital because social norms must somehow be transmitted. Cultural values are transmitted not only from parents to children or peer to peer but also through extended family, neighbors, and other non-family members associated with educational, religious, and other cultural and social activities. Voluntary association is one mechanism of action through which social learning becomes social capital.

Clubs, churches, mosques, temples, unions, and other formal associations create lives that are meaningful, self-actualizing, and enjoyable. Individuals, according to Edmund Burke and other social philosophers, benefit from belonging to a "platoon," a link between family and society. Our lives and the lives of others

---

[1] Alberto Alesina and Paola Giuliano, "Culture and Institutions," *Journal of Economic Literature* 53, no. 4 (Fall 2015): 898–944.

are enriched by this participation. Isolation, freely chosen, has its place, but, in general, the lives of those lacking social ties, regardless of income, are somewhat grim and impoverished. Individuals are motivated to join clubs and participate in service agencies to improve their well-being. The fruit or by-product of rightly ordered associations are *positive externalities* (benefits that accrue to others) that build social capital and contribute to the common good.

A Sense of Purpose and Belonging

Fraternal organizations such as Elks, Knights of Columbus, and Rotary clubs, no longer play a dominant role in American cultural life. Nevertheless, they offer a template for social capital formation by describing characteristics useful in reviving civil society.

Until the early twentieth century, mutual aid provided through fraternal organizations was the social cornerstone for approximately a third of American households. These associations organized health and burial benefits, and others established orphanages, hospitals, job exchanges, homes for the elderly, and scholarships.

As nongovernmental organizations, mutuals operated to advance solidarity but in a way that discouraged dependency and instead fostered self-reliance, business training, thrift, leadership skills, self-government, self-control, and moral character. Social capital is created when such values, practiced and transmitted, build consensus and allow for collective decision-making cutting across seemingly intractable divisions such as race, sex, and income.

The historian David Beito studied five fraternal societies thriving around the turn of the twentieth century. Two of these associations, the Independent Order of Saint Luke and the United Order of True Reformers, consisted exclusively of black membership. The Loyal Order of Moose, emphasizing sickness and burial benefits, was limited to males, but the Security Benefit

Association (originally the Knights and Ladies of Security) offered membership to men and women on equal terms. Finally, the Ladies of the Maccabees, an all-white, all-female society, provided health benefits, including surgical care.[2]

Although personal benefits were no doubt the primary motivation for seeking membership, what each organization held in common, according to Beito, was an emphasis on self-reliance. Therefore, members were expected to be economically self-reliant and gain proficiency in the arts of cooperation and leadership. Formative benefits included self-discipline and personal achievements, but these qualities were tempered with an expectation of civility and reciprocity. A vigilant watch was maintained over those who endangered harmony within the lodge by indulging in personal attacks. To widen the applicant pool, nonpartisan membership was preferred, and all five societies prohibited income and class distinctions. Better educated and more affluent members were more likely to be leaders, but it was not unusual for a "modest workingman" to direct meetings attended by his or her employers who were co-members.

Although the objectives of these fraternal organizations were expressed in similar terminology, the interpretation and application of their mission diverged. Therefore, each found creative ways to customize such ideals as thrift, self-reliance, and self-government to suit the special needs and interests of members. For example, the United Order of True Reformers and the Independent Order of Saint Luke created programs to advance the standing of the black community.

By the 1930s, fraternal societies had entered a period of decline from which they never recovered. Beito's analysis of the decline helps pinpoint a parallel decline in social capital. Like

---

[2] David Beito, "From Mutual Aid to Welfare State: How Fraternal Societies Fought Poverty and Taught Character," Heritage Foundation, July 27, 2000, https://www.heritage.org/political-process/report/mutual-aid-welfare-state-how-fraternal-societies-fought-poverty-and-taught.

Putnam, he attributes some of the change to the lure of newer forms of entertainment, such as radio and movies. As government assistance replaced mutual aid, Beito concludes, fraternal organizations were transformed into providers of insurance policies and recreation available elsewhere.

The high degree of social capital characterized by fraternal societies builds on existing levels of trust between individuals relating to one another. However, organizations in and of themselves matter. Private organizations, including schools, social service agencies, and clubs, are not a sufficient condition for creating and maintaining social capital but are an indispensable means for practicing nonfamily collective decision-making.

Some Evidence Supporting Early Participation with Life-Long Social Capital

There are few studies linking the effects of organizational participation on social capital. Here, we can present two but must qualify that each study was sponsored by the organization being evaluated. In both cases, a survey of former participants was used to determine whether the purported objectives of the organizations were realized. Self-studies, whatever their limitations, are one means of identifying how an organization contributes over the long run to the stock of social capital.

The 4-H, a public-private partnership, engages youth in clubs across the United States. Pennsylvania State University's Department of Agriculture and Extension Services cooperated in a survey that examines the contribution of 4-H on the personal development of 4-H alumni in Pennsylvania (see table 3). The authors of the study conclude that self-reported 4-H experiences greatly contributed to respondents' developing group interaction, leadership, and decision-making skills.[3]

---

[3] A total of 168 out of a random sample of 289 4-H alumni responded to a mail survey. Respondents, 74 percent female, had participated in 4-H an average of 8.5 years.

Table 3
A Survey of Former Participants:
How 4-H Participation Affected Personal Development

Statement	n	M*	SD	Rank
Developing personal pride in achievements and progress	165	6.19	1.08	1
Enjoying recreation, leisure, companionship, fun	164	6.00	1.14	2
Developing self-esteem/self confidence	164	5.96	1.22	3
Setting and working to achieve personal goals	165	5.81	1.20	4
Building group interaction skills	164	5.68	1.32	5
Acquiring skills for leadership	163	5.61	1.65	6
Developing decision making skills	163	5.60	1.29	7
Learning skills for judging, evaluating, and assessing	163	5.59	1.60	8
Acquiring teamwork skills	163	5.58	1.40	9
Building leadership skills	163	5.58	1.67	10
Developing problem solving skills	163	5.50	1.24	11
Learning meeting management skills/democratic procedures	164	5.41	1.68	12
Acquiring skills necessary for employment	163	5.19	1.60	13
Practicing good habits of health, fitness, and safety	164	4.89	1.60	14
Learning money management	165	4.74	1.69	15
Acquiring and developing good nutritional practices	164	4.68	1.70	16
Learning business management skills and techniques	163	4.60	1.61	17
Developing entrepreneurial skills	162	4.59	1.84	18

*Mean computed on a scale 1 (no contribution) to 7 (great contribution)

Source: Rama B. Radhakrishna and Megan Sinasky, "4-H Experiences Contributing to Leadership and Personal Development of 4-H Alumni," Journal of Extension 43, no. 6 (December 2005), www.joe.org.

Boy Scouts of America, like 4-H, commissioned a survey of former members. Harris Interactive conducted the survey and produced the report, *Values of Americans: A Study of Ethics and Character*, to examine the ethics and character of Americans—young and old—to compare changes in norms over time, and to assess one organization's long-term influence on behavior.[4]

The first section of the survey compares the attitudes of adult men and women with males and females in fourth through twelfth grades. Unfortunately, changes in attitudes over time are unavailable because data for females was not part of the initial 1995 survey. However, the 2005 results suggest that women more strongly oppose unethical behavior than do men.

The second section of the *Values of Americans* study, dealing exclusively with men and boys, does permit comparisons between 1995 and 2005. As compared with the 1995 survey, fewer men responding to the 2005 survey placed high importance on showing concern for their neighbors' property, keeping their property clean and tidy, or attending religious services regularly. Measures of ethical beliefs also declined. Fewer men agreed that being honest with everyone pays off and that preserving our environment for future generations is very important. Fewer men thought it wrong under all circumstances to smoke marijuana, and slightly more reported using this drug. American values related to ethical behaviors varied according to the perceived degree of the offense. Respondents to the later survey continued to indicate strong opposition to the illicit use of hard drugs such as heroin or LSD but held more lenient views on taking office supplies for personal use or speeding on the road.

---

[4] *Values of Americans* consists of three distinct but interrelated summaries based on a random telephone sample of 1,524 US adults and a paper survey distributed randomly to 1,714 youth attending public, private, and parochial schools across the United States.

Youth respondents appear to value honesty and ethical behavior. Most would not participate in dishonest or destructive acts, and very few reported participating in acts such as carrying a gun to school, using hard drugs such as LSD, or shoplifting. However, like adults, they tend to participate in dishonest or unethical acts that they feel carry fewer consequences or are a response to peer pressure, such as cheating on homework or tests and drinking alcohol. Almost one in five youth participated in binge drinking or fighting. It should also be noted that participating in these destructive or unethical behaviors increased with age. Comparing youth in 1995 to youth in 2005 reveals some encouraging trends. Fewer youth reported shoplifting, cheating on homework, carrying a gun to school, or being a member of a gang.

The final section of the survey presented in figure 1 enables us to compare the perceptions of adult men in general and former scouts concerning certain behaviors. Men with scouting backgrounds were more likely than those with no scouting background to place greater importance on measures of good citizenship. This was especially true of men who were scouts for five or more years. Men who were scouts believed that voting in every election, showing concern for their neighbor's property, keeping their property clean and tidy, and staying physically fit are essential to good citizenship. Men with scouting backgrounds also gave greater importance to attending church or religious services regularly, financially supporting religious organizations, participating in youth-related organizations, taking part in charitable organizations, and volunteering time in the community.

Percent Saying Absolutely Essential	All Scouts	Scout 5+ Years	Never a Scout
Vote in every election	40%	47%	29%
Showing concern for your neighbor's property	33%	37%	24%
Keeping one's property clean and tidy	24%	28%	23%
Keeping informed on current events	25%	26%	21%
Keeping physically fit	19%	25%	21%
Attending religious services regularly	18%	22%	14%
Giving financial support to religious organizations	15%	19%	12%
Participating in youth-related organizations	12%	17%	10%
Taking an active part in charitable organizations	11%	15%	10%
Volunteering time in the community	10%	13%	11%

Figure 1. Behaviors That American Adult Males Surveyed Indicate as Being Essential

Based on the responses of 595 men who were Scouts as a youth; 248 men who were Scouts 5+ years; 410 non-Scouts.

Source: Values of Americans: A Study of Ethics and Character, Harris Interactive Report Produced by Boy Scouts of America Youth and Family Research Center, May 2005, https://filestore.scouting.org/filestore/marketing/pdf/02-849.pdf.

Both the 4-H and Scouting studies indicate that formal intermediaries recognize and seek to justify their roles in stemming the tide of decreased social capital. Both organizations, characterized by an internal hierarchy, a division of labor, and functional distinctions, contribute to social capital. This recognition by the organizations of their role in social capital formation raises the question of why many Americans have lost faith in formal organizations and continue to reduce their participation.

Not All Intermediaries Contribute to Social Capital

Although we have thus far emphasized the benefits of local organization and institutions, it must be conceded that these are not in all cases forces for good. In less affluent neighborhoods, social networks are much more likely to transmit social dysfunction than to provide solutions. Even churches, often the last surviving community organizations, are vulnerable to adverse neighborhood influences.[5] Why have private intermediaries, including those sponsored by churches, not been able to shield themselves from the dysfunction present in their social and cultural environment? Indeed, it appears in some instances that these organizations are responsible for the breakdown of trust, which is the mortar between the civic bricks consisting of religious institutions, athletic teams, social service agencies, and miscellaneous volunteer activities.

The failings of private intermediaries must be seriously addressed. Of concern is the fact that individuals participating in voluntary organizations experience disappointment, betrayal, being taken for granted, dismissed, and misunderstood. To an extent, these are the ordinary ups and downs of participation within any family, business, or voluntary organization. On the other hand, these problems sometimes rise to abusive—even criminal—levels such as in the cases of pedophiles and other

---

[5] Putnam, *Our Kids*, 206.

corrupt actors working in tax-exempt organizations that purport to act in trust for those unable to fend for themselves. Unfortunately, this behavior is all too common and an issue about which economists, unlike attorneys, have little expertise.

Economists, however, do offer some insight into organizations, including those that are dysfunctional and thus failing to contribute to social capital formation. A *negative internality* is a concept useful in analyzing organizational dysfunction arising within organizations.

Research on negative internalities attempts to demonstrate how internal governance is distorted by improperly aligned incentives. Social capital is created when incentives are aligned to ensure that administrators, employees, clients, and other stakeholders do not use influence, assertiveness, or self-deception to advance the personal interests of one individual or a subset of stakeholders.

Social service agencies tend to survive indefinitely. This is the case even when unresponsive to clients and incapable of moving toward consistent objectives. Measures of output, quality, and effectiveness are hard to define in the not-for-profit sector. Feedback from clients is often lacking or unreliable. Therefore, nonmarket agencies often assume internal procedures and practices that lack a clear or reliable connection with the ostensible public purpose that the organizations were intended to serve.[6]

Intermediaries have revenue streams other than direct payments received from clients; thus, the list of potential negative internalities is endless. For example, an organization, social club, or social agency that has been co-opted and functions as a cooperative for its staff, fails both its members and clients. Also, if any one source of revenue is threatened, an intermedi-

---

[6] Charles Wolf, Jr., "A Theory of Nonmarket Failure: Framework for Implementation Analysis," *Journal of Law & Economics* 22, no. 1 (1979): 117.

ary may opt to offer commercial or other services unrelated to its primary mission. An endowment can be used to increase or guarantee employee salaries rather than provide social services. To maintain a revenue source, resources are sometimes shifted internally to meet targets and indicators not necessarily associated with good service. Consequently, when social services are provided cooperatively through private intermediaries, donors, administrators, board members, professionals, and staff need to be on the same page, so to speak, concerning mission, values, and rules of exchange.

Negative externalities, differing from negative internalities, deal with the transmission of social dysfunction beyond the organization. When private organizations produce negative externalities, the deep cultural bonds extending to society at large are threatened. One of the most important cultural bonds is generalized trust toward others; that is, how people respond to those they do not know personally. Not every private intermediary creates generalized trust extending to society at large. Catholic social teaching warns against autonomous organizations operating by blind impulse without regard for loyalty and the common good. As Benedict XVI insisted, the valid "autonomy of intermediate bodies" must be balanced by the principle of solidarity—a commitment to the good of all—so that individual organizations do not fall into "social privatism."[7]

Negative externalities arise in certain instances when the degree of internal cohesiveness is exceedingly high but the organization is focused on goals contrary to the well-being of society as a whole. Such organizations decrease the degree to which members trust outsiders and work effectively with them. Highly disciplined, well-organized groups sharing strong common values are capable of highly coordinated collective action but

---

[7] Pope Benedict XVI, Encyclical Letter *Caritas in Veritate* (2009), nos. 57–58.

function as a social liability. These organizations can effectively employ their accumulated social capital to transmit negative externalities; at worst, they actively breed distrust, intolerance, or even hatred for and violence toward outsiders.[8]

Criminal organizations, gangs, and various self-regarding ethnic and racial organizations score high in internal trust and can be quite effective in achieving their collective goals. In these cases, general welfare is at risk, and officials are required to make judgments regarding monitoring or banning organizations they believe to be acting against the public interest. However, care must be taken not to undermine the protection of institutions that have a constitutional right to exist.

Given intermediary organizations' potential for social dysfunction, it could be argued that positive externalities transmitted by private organizations are minimal. Some hold that the interests and values of individuals are too much at odds with a cooperative effort extending beyond a small network of family and kin. To support this assumption, they refer to experimental studies indicating that when members of various groups are combined, participants are more willing to share and cooperate with in-group members than out-group members. Therefore, they argue that social services are better financed, provided, and distributed by the government.

It is indeed unrealistic to assume that persons associated with not-for-profit organizations consistently pursue mission objectives or consistently use social capital to benefit society at large. Why, then, are voluntary organizations, which are so vulnerable to negative internalities and negative externalities, tolerated and even encouraged? To paraphrase Winston Churchill's famous aphorism on democratic government, private organizations may be the worst way of building social capital—except for all the other ways that have been tried.

---

[8] Fukuyama, "Social Capital," 431

Compared to other methods, private voluntary organizations are a low-cost, effective means of accumulating social capital. Their effectiveness can be enhanced and the possibility of dysfunction diminished by employing self-correcting feedback loops for limiting dysfunctional organizational behavior.

How do these self-correcting feedback loops operate? By threatening membership decline and loss of financial support, cross-monitoring by diverse stakeholders works to keep organizations on track. Similarly, a responsive government ensures that private organizations operate in the public interest. The *necessary* condition, however, for these feedback loops to operate, is that organizational stakeholders and community residents embody social capital.

VI Requirements for Growth in Social Capital

The image of unmotivated millennials on the computer in their parents' basements rather than attending class, holding jobs, or forming families may or may not be a fair or accurate characterization. Like homeschooling and homebirths, this behavior could represent a lack of trust in or familiarity with existing institutions. Perhaps the long-term net effect of social media and "sharing" platforms will be increased social capital. However, Fukuyama's concern with networks of trust, Putnam's observations on declining participation, and Murray's pinpointing of social dysfunction are serious issues if social capital—the capacity to work together to achieve common objectives—continues to decline.

In *Our Kids*, Robert Putnam describes Kensington, a dangerous neighborhood in Philadelphia. Older adults still living there recall childhoods oriented around a local recreation club, a skating rink, parks, public pools, sports teams, and dances sponsored by fraternal organizations and the city's department of recreation. But today, crime is pervasive; police no longer walk the beat and people keep to themselves.[1] Kensington's degeneration is associated with increased single parenting, joblessness, and detachment from religious and other institutions.

---

[1] Putname, *Our Kids*, 200.

Contrary to a romanticized image of close-knit communal life among the poor, it is better-educated Americans who have wider and deeper social networks or are better able to compensate for their lack. Lower-class Americans tend to remain socially isolated from extended family and neighbors.[2] Tocqueville saw the ever-present danger in a democratic society that certain groups would gain the power to take away from people the faculty of modifying their lot. This danger would result in dependence on an inflexible providence or a feeling of blind fatality.[3] We see in the United States a growing underclass living in "noncommunities" with few functional social organizations.

It may be the case that declining social capital and dependence on government are not exclusively lower-income phenomena. Increasing suicide rates are not necessarily associated with income. Higher income families certainly can afford to purchase private services for their children, minimizing the negative consequences of drugs and other misadventures. Regardless of income, however, everyone needs a degree of social connectedness in order to achieve one's goals.[4] It is important to emphasize that social capital formation is not an issue of social networking (who you know) or learning to be self-assertive but rather one of embedding social capabilities through active participation.

---

[2] Putnam, *Our Kids*, 207

[3] Clarence Thomas, "Victims and Heroes in the 'Benevolent State,'" in *Morality and Moral Controversies*, John Arthur, ed. (Upper Saddle River, NJ: Prentice Hall, 1999), 565.

[4] Putnam, *Our Kids*, 210.

Democracy and the Freedom of Association

The First Amendment of the US Constitution guarantees the right of citizens to assemble peaceably and petition government. Catholic social teaching does not specify constitutional rights but indicates that authentic democracy allows for and requires the creation of structures for participation and shared responsibility (*CA*, no. 46). Although the liberty to associate freely seems natural, each generation must be reminded of its importance. Social capital is attained by individuals freely associating, but the survival of the democratic state, itself a voluntary association, requires social capital.

Those seeking to control all aspects of society are willing to dispense with the freedom to associate. Thinking that they possess the secret for perfection—making evil impossible—they are often willing to use any means, including violence and deceit, to bring their vision into being (*CA*, no. 25). In this way, an all-powerful state or party tends to absorb the nation, society, all private organizations, and individuals themselves (*CA*, no. 45).

Although there remains a "well-nigh irresistible urge in man to combine with his fellows for the attainment of aims and objectives which are beyond the means or capabilities of single individuals," we observe the growing intervention of the state in social life, "even in matters which are of intimate concern to the individual" (*MM*, no. 60).

Whose job is it to guarantee freedom of association? The primary responsibility belongs not to an abstract state but rather to individuals and various groups imbued with social capital. Any state intervention into society must be brief and avoid enlarging the state to the detriment of both economic and civil freedom (*CA*, no. 48).

We admit to a tautological problem. Democracy and effective private organizations require social capital, but social capital formation requires liberty and the freedom to associate. Therefore, the social capital required for a well-functioning democracy cannot be created by excluding and denying autonomy to organizations, particularly those founded on the principles of morality, law, culture, and religion (*CA*, no. 19).

From Passivity to Self-Reliance

Catholic social teaching assumes that there is a natural inclination for rational creatures to participate in providing for themselves and others. However, this natural tendency can be thwarted. State intervention "brings with it a multiplicity of restrictive laws and regulations in many departments of human life. As a consequence, it narrows the sphere of a person's freedom of action." Invasive procedures "conspire to make it difficult for a person to think independently of outside influences, to act on his own initiative, exercise his responsibility and express and fulfill his own personality." Government alone is not responsible for diminished self-reliance. If intermediary organizations are to be the main vehicle for social capital formation, their effectiveness can only be realized "if they treat their individual members as human persons and encourage them to take an active part in the ordering of their lives" (*MM*, nos. 62, 65).

Beito lists factors indicating how voluntary reciprocity slowly gave way to paternalistic dependency. First, the medical profession imposed sanctions, including denial of licenses, against doctors who contracted with fraternal organizations. Second, the twentieth century brought unprecedented expansion in government-provided welfare. Finally, post-World War II employer-provided fringe benefits, including health insurance, were exempted from income tax, encouraging companies to offer benefits that had previously been the purview of mutual aid societies. Thus personal identities and well-being in the United States became more closely identified with government and employers. This transformed identity reduced the incentives of individuals to participate in voluntary organizations.

Requirements for Growth in Social Capital

When individuals become passive, civic society withers—except for groups advocating increased public services. Unfortunately, we may have reached a point at which it has become prohibitively expensive to privately offer a certain level of social services, including health insurance and education, because unlimited provision is now perceived and promised as a legal right. Government provision of social services has become more common, but quality may not be greater. Dense social networks in older urban neighborhoods provided for cleanliness, minimization of street crime, and other quality-of-life measures to a higher degree than more formal institutions.[5]

The concept of *moral hazard* assists in understanding dependency and its relationship to declining social capital. Moral hazard refers to the likelihood of a person failing to comply with expected behavior as contracted. For example, those in the insurance industry are aware that inappropriate incentives cause clients to shift their behavior and become more careless. Moral hazard adversely affects the allocation of resources to those truly in need due to circumstances beyond their control. When moral hazard exists on a large scale, it transmits negative externalities, increasing costs and harming third parties beyond the client/agency relationship.

Organizations, too, are adversely affected by moral hazard when expected to assume all costs and responsibility for student learning, medical care, counseling, and other social services. In other words, a recipient no longer needs to strive to the extent he or she is capable. The client-recipient has less incentive to become a contributing partner or to assist in preserving a particular culture. In other words, recipients have no purpose other than to be passive receivers of whatever minimum amount of service it is that an agency is willing to provide in order to maintain its source of revenue.

---

[5] Fukuyama, "Social Capital," 377.

Rebuilding Social Capital

Individuals in distress, or merely seeking service, are often treated in ways inconsistent with their capacities as human beings to act purposefully on their own behalf. In some cases, even an applicant is viewed as a victim and personally incompetent. Thus, those offering services overreach in attempting to direct the lives of clients. Clients in need of short-term, focused assistance available through a monopolistic provider, are faced with a choice: They can either forgo service or permit their capabilities for assuming personal responsibility to atrophy. In these instances, agencies become facilitators of behavior detrimental to clients, organizations, and society as a whole.

Clients, of course, should not permit themselves to be perceived as dependents reducible to a rat-like response to stimuli. However, they often need reminders that membership and service are not without costs to someone. Aside from fees and dues, affiliation and service must be earned through a willingness to cooperate with treatment and organizational procedures. Intermediate institutions require the ability to firmly resist domination by clients or any other stakeholder seeking to co-opt the organization. We are suggesting that social capital is optimally created when organizations and their member/clients view the process as a cooperative in which each of the primary stakeholders has voice and standing.

Social services, including leisure activities, have increasingly become characterized by impersonal bureaucracies funded by tax revenue. Eligibility depends not on any reciprocal or participatory activity but rather on a growing list of perceived rights. These organizations focus not on clients but on professional grantsmanship. Social capital formation requires a different approach.

Over time, informal and formal institutions evolve to handle changing norms and priorities. It is unknown, however, how long it will take or what mechanisms will be put in place to effectively deal with present social crises. Meanwhile, the goal should be to forge a social equilibrium through a multitude of private intermediaries. This framework is consistent with democratic government in a pluralistic society. In the virtual space located between family and state, individuals can voluntarily cooperate in dealing with uncertainty, distress, and the pursuit of happiness. America has relied on high schools, colleges, and even the military draft to provide an all-inclusive package of academic, social, aesthetic, athletic, and other experiences. As teens and young adults reduce or postpone on-site attendance at these institutions, substitute organizations will be seen as critical for social capital formation.

Universities generally do not attempt to manage professionals through detailed bureaucratic work rules. Similarly, personnel in other firms employing highly educated workers are trusted to be self-managing by internalizing professional standards. Professional education is consequently a major source of social capital in any advanced, postindustrial society. Trust provides the basis for decentralized, flat organizations. Authority does not disappear in a flat or networked organization; rather, it is internalized in a way that permits self-organization and self-management.[6] There is no reason, however, to assume that professionals hold a patent on cooperative skills. Social capital can be embedded in any group of individuals free and willing to associate with each other to achieve a common goal. Consider the self-organization and self-management required for setting up childcare cooperatives, organizing golf and tennis clubs, and initiating enrichment activities.

Clients and club members assume the risk of uncertain outcomes. For example, with respect to education and social services, individuals freely submit themselves to a process without guaranteed results. However, in dealing with vulnerable clients, those choosing and those delivering the service do not bear the

---

[6] Fukuyama, "Social Capital," 446.

consequences. Certain recipients, particularly children and the seriously mentally and physically impaired, are unable to evaluate the quality or appropriateness of a given service. They depend on advocates, highly trained professionals, and organizations to act in trust for them. This trust factor is one, if not the primary, justification for a variety of intermediaries.[7] Ideally, multiple providers vie for clientele. Clients or their advocates assume responsibility for differentiating between contenders offering similar services.

In the United States, parents generally are granted the standing to make choices for dependent children. The expectation is that individuals formed with values embedded in them by family and culture will choose well. However, freedom is not free, and outcomes are not guaranteed. Therefore, in differentiating between social, medical, and educational providers, clients pay for information on quality. They do this with time spent observing the experience of others and/or by indirectly assuming the costs of accreditation by independent standard-setting organizations. Social networks reduce the search costs of acquiring information and offer assistance in discovering the best fit for particular needs. Through this process, persons come to realize that no public or private agency can eliminate uncertainty and to gain confidence in assuming responsibility for making good choices.

That clients are capable of self-direction and free will is not an illusion, a myth to be discarded. Over time, personal responsibility has been deemphasized.[8] Hopelessness about the meaning of life, a breakdown in the social/institutional framework, and increased emotional fragility in coping with uncertainty are

---

[7] Henry B. Hansmann, "The Effect of Tax Exemption and Other Factors on the Market Share of Nonprofit Versus For-Profit Firms," *National Tax Journal* 40 (March 1987): 71–82.

[8] Tibor Machan, *Initiative, Human Agency, and Society* (Stanford, CA: Hoover Institution Press, 2000).

just a few of the negative consequences resulting from lowered expectations about the ability of individuals to choose well. If we are seriously concerned about declining social capital, each policy proposal will be evaluated in terms of the choice and responsibility reserved for individuals or, when appropriate, their designated agents.

VII Reawakening a Vibrant Civic Sector

Catholic social teaching in the past focused on employee unions and government to remediate social problems. Changing production skills and consumption patterns requires a continual effort to retrain and mediate employment practices. However, the current fundamental problem may be more social than occupational as people crowd into cities around the world and lack the family and cultural roots to assist them in becoming socially integrated.

With increasing percentages of children growing up in single-parent households, the government has intervened to mitigate distress. Some would argue this intervention has facilitated shifting norms contributing to social dysfunction. In any case, it has become apparent that the state has not been very successful in performing socialization functions traditionally assumed by other smaller-scale groups, and government attempts to perform these functions come at great economic cost.

The Private Advantage in Creating Social Capital

When individuals are inclined to associate freely, the spontaneous result is a civil society consisting of a network of social providers located in the public space between government and families. Intermediaries do not subsume the role of families and the firms in which they earn a living but rather act as a necessary buffer between the individual and the state. On a micro level, each particular intermediary is a voluntary cooperative effort on the part of stakeholders to realize a perceived mission. The goal of such nonprofit organizations is not to advocate for more tax revenue or get votes but rather to be effective.

Efficiency and competition are associated with for-profit firms, a subset of nongovernment organizations in need of liberty to achieve their goals. In contrast, voluntary cooperation in not-for-profit organizations seeks effectiveness, not efficiency. Friedrich Hayek, noted Nobel Prize economist, attributes much of his work in market economics to Lord Acton and Tocqueville, known for their acute insights into society as a whole. Hayek reminds us that society is far more complex than many realize. Expertise in business, education, medicine, and alleviating human distress is dispersed among millions of individuals. The task of social science is to demonstrate how little is known by those who imagine they can design the good life for customers, clients, or hobbyists.[1]

Because many social services are generally unavailable in the marketplace, people band together to collectively subsidize and offer them. However, such services can be delivered in corporate for-profit settings, in voluntary nonprofit institutions, or by government. Observing the pervasive unintended and sometimes tragic consequences of educational, medical, and welfare policies, it is puzzling as to why, in modern, culturally diverse, affluent societies, the government is often chosen to monopolistically finance, produce, and deliver social services.

Privately sponsored and subsidized intermediaries, such as private schools, charitable organizations, women's care centers, the Salvation Army, the YMCA, Boy and Girls' Clubs, homeless and prisoner release shelters, and soup kitchens are just a few of the organizations offering social services. Fraternal organi-

---

[1] Hayek, *Road to Serfdom*.

zations such as the Knights of Columbus, Shriners, Habitat, Doctors Without Borders, Alcoholics Anonymous, Elks, and Parents Without Partners also assist individuals and families given the inevitable uncertainties of the human condition. The effectiveness of what appears to be a hodgepodge of diverse intermediaries compares favorably to a sole government provider. Government agencies often produce a standard or substandard level of service and lack the flexibility to innovate and change course.

Certainly, government social agencies operating in stable, culturally homogeneous societies are more effective and less likely to be harmful. However, pluralistic societies are characterized by significant migration, less extended family support, and economic disruption. Subgroups assign a different weighting to various social norms and customs. The greater the likelihood of subgroups holding different values or experiencing distress, the greater the need for a variety of social intermediaries flexible enough to address personal contingencies and avoid social chaos. Government bureaucracies, particularly in pluralistic societies, have high transaction costs associated with adapting their services to different communities.

Solving social problems through collective political action is challenging because cultural values are deeply embedded in diverse groups and alterable, if at all, only slowly and at the margin.[2] Government policy goals are set in legislative assemblies, far removed from agencies delivering services and twice removed from the priorities and aspirations of client-recipients. This is not necessarily a criticism of government, which must be accountable to taxpayers financing services. Rather, it is a recognition of the inadequate tools available to government in

---

[2] "Why Government Fails So Often: And How It Can Do Better," Book Forum video featuring Peter Schuck, Cato Institute, April 13, 2014, https://www.cato.org/events/why-government-fails-so-often-how-it-can-do-better.

determining value for individuals with different priorities over a range of services.

Benefits produced by any social service agency are difficult to assess. Therefore, we default to a single inadequate indicator: the number or dollar value of inputs used. Other proxies for benefits include average time allocated per case by social workers, dollars allocated per student, class size, research papers published, and clients served per professional. These are remote proxies for the "real" or final amount of service received by clients.

Service quality is also elusive. Stakeholders generally insist that agencies pursue multiple mandates. Information, automatically transmitted by customers paying full price in profit-seeking firms, is lacking. Consider, for example, adoption services, foster homes, retirement communities, and schools. Generally, a client does not pay the full cost, donors do not personally experience the service, and advocates act in trust for client recipients. Consider the impossible task of determining whether the quality of a given program or curriculum is "better" or "worse" following a policy change. When a single agency is providing service, the probability of being effective decreases.[3]

A strong social support network, as compared with specialized treatment, is associated with better adjustment to stressful events.[4] However, those who are physically or mentally unable to cope tend to be socially isolated. Therefore, easy access to professional expertise is critical for those unable to maintain social ties. A diversity of organizations offers more opportunities for caregivers to develop administrative capabilities and flexibility in targeting services.

Cost-benefit analysis (CBA) remains the best quantitative tool presently available to assess the worthiness of social projects.

---

[3] Wolf, "A Theory of Nonmarket Failure," 113.

[4] Dora L. Costa and Matthew E. Kahn, *Heroes & Cowards: The Social Face of War* (Princeton: Princeton University Press, 2008).

Cost-benefit analysis methodology ignores residents who may be ineligible or incapable of realizing benefits.[5] With CBA, all individual goals are collapsed into one goal. For example, the goal of state subsidies to higher education is often reduced to comparing total tax revenue from students' future earnings with taxpayer costs. Social programs can meet the cost-benefit criterion yet fail to address deep cultural and social needs.

Discontent with social services affects democracy. It leads to the erroneous assumption that experts, permanent officials, or independent, autonomous bodies can circumvent politics.[6] In the United States, "Common Core" for K–12 education and "Affordable Care" in medicine represent the disconnect between government's inability to deliver service and hope, versus the expectation that experts on the federal level will succeed.

Irreconcilable differences on what and how services should be provided cannot be resolved by general rules. One option is to permit a local authority using the force of law to make arbitrary decisions. This option demands that government act in full knowledge of harmful redistributive effects to certain groups. If constituents object, officials—not teachers, social workers, or clients—rule. "Fair" or "reasonable" government provision depends unrealistically on nothing short of complete knowledge of the value of satisfying every want of every person or group.[7]

Private intermediaries target a particular level of provision, subject to available resources. But public agencies are expected to meet all needs, an impossible task. When services are denied, reduced, or misallocated by public agencies, interest groups act strategically to redirect services to themselves. Residents relo-

---

[5] David Levy and Sandra J. Peart, "Learning from Failure: A Review of Peter Schuck's *Why Government Fails So Often: And How It Can Do Better*," *Journal of Economic Literature* 53, no. 3 (2015): 669.

[6] Hayek, *Road to Serfdom*, 65.

[7] Hayek, *Road to Serfdom*, 81.

cate rather than be taxed for services they do not value. Those that cannot move are trapped into dependent relationships with monopolistic suppliers. Understandably, a lack of trust in democracy in general and existing institutions, or confidence in our abilities to change them, leads to resentment and social disruption.

When social services are delivered through government agencies as compared with private intermediaries, social isolation increases and social capital declines. There is a need to refocus attention on giving individuals, particularly clients in need of social services, a sense of belonging and participation. This refocusing requires processing needs as close to the source as possible and effectively utilizing the widely dispersed skills that are lying dormant in our respective disciplines and traditions.

Avoiding Organizational Failure

For many Americans today, there are fewer and fewer enduring loves, demanding loyalties, and cultural ties. Fewer people live where they were born. Families are less stable. Individuals become self-absorbed. This takes place against a background of perpetual dissatisfaction and critiquing of institutions. Families are not seen as refuges in a cruel world but rather as the source of psychological distress. Organized religion is considered fantasy, and patriotism, foolish.[8] In this environment, restoring trust in intermediaries is an uphill battle.

The pedophilia crisis in the Catholic Church and elsewhere, deaths due to hazing in college fraternities, lack of transparency in admission procedures, and other egregious examples of abuse suggest that private organizations are not exempt from the kinds of failures also found in government. Criminal behavior, co-optation by employees, administrative perks, careerism,

---

[8] R. R. Reno "False Freedom," *First Things*, October 2015, https://www.firstthings.com/article/2015/10/false-freedom.

bureaucratic bloat, rent-seeking, voting paradoxes, inappropriate measures of effectiveness, and indifference to clients are found in all types of formal organizations. Such negative internalities are inevitable and must be recognized and addressed in clubs and agencies claiming to act in trust for members and clients.

The issue addressed here, however, is that opportunities for building social capital are not found in large bureaucracies or professionally operated foundations. Nor are they found in "mailing list" organizations such as the American Association of Retired Persons or the Sierra Club. These organizations are designed for people with common sympathies but not necessarily social connectedness. Members of mailing-list organizations contribute yearly dues and receive a newsletter but have little reason for cooperating with one another on issues unrelated to advocating for benefits. Nominal membership and social media platforms, however valuable, are not perfect substitutes for participation in member-controlled organizations. Private institutions create social value by encouraging beneficial internal rules of an exchange, not by positioning the organization externally to gain an advantage.[9]

Administrative mandates suppress individual freedom. This is not a serious concern if individuals are free to create new organizations, exit existing ones, attempt to get their particular views adopted—or simply acquiesce, if they wish. Through private but formal associations, individuals learn to value contracts, rules of order, constitutions, and mission statements. As they become better at judging who and what to trust, they themselves may choose to be trustworthy and to share valuable information with other participants.

---

[9] Vernon Smith, *Constructivist and Ecological Rationality in Economics: Nobel Prize Lecture*, (Fairfax, VA: George Mason University, 2002).

A constant interchange of thought, experience, valuable feedback, and the substantial benefits from cooperation substitute for a common world view. Because the probability of agreement on a particular course of action decreases as the scope of the organization is extended, optimal size must be taken into account depending on the type of service offered. In any organization, when individuals disagree, practical unanimity or a substantial majority is required to proceed, in full knowledge that some stakeholders may be negatively affected. Those working in the field of social services are a contentious lot, but even they realize that common effort breaks down when opinions approach the number of participants!

Vigilance on the part of sponsors and donors along with the constant interchange of thought help in arresting negative internalities. Sponsors can insist on benchmarking service quality; benchmarking is a process of identifying, understanding, and adopting effective practices from anywhere in the world. Analyzing superior performance in furthering the mission, rather than pursuing the objectives of particular stakeholders, is the best means of learning what works and what does not. This analysis permits an organization to self-correct and change course.

Are there any fail-safe procedures to keep private intermediaries on track regarding institutional mission? There are no good substitutes aside from offering choice in providers. And, whenever possible, it is best to subsidize clients rather than institutions delivering services. The private institutional sector, lacking a steady stream of tax revenue, is subject to the free entry and exit of social service providers—and this is good. Unless a private institution's services are valued enough to be voluntarily paid for or subsidized by donors, it will and should cease to exist.

Institutions, sponsored by either church or state, that deviate from mission or foster dependency thereby fail to promote personal development and social capital. Private intermediaries with clearly specified mission statements, unlike government bureaucracies, are designed to assist individuals in unique circumstances. Individuals and families should be free to move between a variety of differentiated providers suitable to their age and other social and economic characteristics. No longer trapped in dependent intrusive relationships, they will be free to select from a cornucopia of services.

Threats to Civil Society

Is civil society at risk? In the first decade of the twenty-first century, private intermediaries actually grew faster than government and business firms with respect to the number of people employed and wages paid. Certainly, not all nonprofit intermediaries are threatened.

Foundations and large national and international organization are growing, whereas private organizations delivering social services, such as schools, adoption services, leisure activities, and other social agencies, show increasing vulnerability. In direct competition with the government, private providers of social services are more numerous than large foundations and public charities, but in general, each receives less revenue and holds fewer assets. On the demand side, the expansion of perceived rights has focused the energies of a population on advocating for increased government provided services. On the supply side, certain types of organizations constituting civil society are discouraged because they interfere with what politicians promise or promote.[10]

Small organizations and clubs engaging in athletic, cultural, and other recreational activities are most at risk for reasons least understood. This risk is unfortunate because such organiza-

---

[10] James Taranto, "What Went Wrong with Human Rights: A Weekend Interview with Aaron Rhodes," *Wall Street Journal*, August 18–19, 2018, A13.

tions have a comparative advantage in creating social capital. A culture of trust cannot be sustained unless people are free to form, directly control, and patronize private intermediaries. Holding aside electronic distractions and the complications of modern lives, what factors in the United States are inhibiting private organizations and adults from participating?

The government in the United States plays a significant role in assisting private organizations. This is done through direct and indirect financial subsidies. It exempts foundations, charities, religious institutions, small clubs, and social service providers from taxes. On a personal level, individuals donating to qualifying organizations earn tax deductions and credits. Furthermore, private organizations, in certain instances, benefit from government grants, subsidized loans, and vouchers.

Of course, with public financing comes accountability to taxpayers along with government oversight to ensure that the social capital created by these activities is directed in ways consistent with the national interest. The justification underlying taxpayer support is that private organizations are producing quasi-public services with positive externalities. The implicit assumption is that government financial support is not to organizations but rather to residents availing themselves of the services and activities privately produced but financed with tax revenue.

Fortunately, the threat to civil intermediaries in the United States, at this time, is not due to overt and systematic government hostility. If the state were to prevent citizens from forming private associations, the very principle of the state's own existence could be questioned.[11] However, official policies, regulations, and funding present serious challenges to private organizations. When government provides even a fraction of operating costs, administrators and users tend to focus on maintaining and increasing the government funding. For example, to maintain

---

[11] Pope Leo XIII, Encyclical Letter *Rerum Novarum* (1891), no. 135.

accreditation not-for-profit administrators must abide by all government regulation. The result is that the primary mission of the sponsoring organization is often subverted and the goals of all other stakeholders subordinated.

Those initiating, for example, an amateur theatre group for teens cannot be expected to possess or pay for the skills of a certified accountant or attorney. It is necessary to address the disincentives experienced by such organizations and, in some cases, hospitable households through which social capital is created. To understand these disincentives, we first consider four extreme cases in which private organizations in the public square can be overtly threatened.

First, private social intermediaries, including schools, hospitals, service agencies, fraternal, and interest organizations, may be entirely banned and declared illegal. Note, however, that some private initiative persists even in tyrannical regimes under which it is prohibited, effectively controlled, or driven underground. Overt prohibition results in declining levels of social trust and increasing levels of crime and public corruption. Similar social pathologies, ironically, can be found in societies such as ours where intermediaries are tolerated but expected to adhere to a strictly prescribed agenda, secular or otherwise.

Second, at times, governments cease to provide those public goods for which it alone holds sovereignty. A dysfunctional government cannot effectively ensure constitutional rights, police protection, and other public goods. In such an environment, civil organizations cannot thrive and the stock of social capital declines.

Third, government discourages the formation of certain types of organizations by differentiating between organizations based on ideological or political bias. In such cases, certain organizations are denied a charter to operate, excluded from tax exemptions, or its donors targeted. The credentials and programs of certain schools, for example, may not be recognized and their graduates prohibited from government employment. There are some recent instances of unjust government discrimination against civil-society organizations, such as a 2016 case involving the Internal Revenue Service's targeting of politically conservative nonprofits, and the revocation of licenses from religious adoption agencies over their unwillingness to place children with same-sex couples.[12]

Finally, excessive rules and regulations become legally binding and require private organizations to engage in a prohibitively costly public and judicial review. The viability of any organization, public or private, is threatened when the per capita cost of providing a service exceeds the per capita payment. Private initiatives are inhibited when very small interest groups are obliged to report modest revenue to the IRS or fear lawsuits potentially resulting in bankruptcy. Confronted with a revenue gap, organizations have an incentive to disband or pursue commercial activities to subsidize their primary mission.

Private voluntary organizations, like free enterprise, require eternal vigilance to remain free. Unfortunately, social services are more controversial than athletic-wear and other consumer goods. Otherwise, a chamber of voluntary organizations would insist on their role as the most effective, least-cost means for creating social capital offering no threat to legitimate democracy.

---

[12] See Matt Zapatosky, "Justice Department Agrees to Settle Lawsuits over IRS Scrutiny of Tea Party Groups," *Washington Post*, October 25, 2017, https://www.washingtonpost.com/world/national-security/justice-department-agrees-to-settle-lawsuits-over-irs-scrutiny-of-tea-party-groups/2017/10/25/519513f8-b9f1-11e7-a908-a3470754bbb9_story.html; and United States Conference of Catholic Bishops, "Discrimination again Catholic Adoption Agencies," USCCB.org, http://www.usccb.org/issues-and-action/religious-liberty/discrimination-against-catholic-adoption-services.cfm.

Meanwhile, the decline in social capital continues, requiring authoritarian government, at some point, to intervene in desperation. Advocates of CST and like-minded groups and individuals must insist on liberty and government's responsibility in creating a safe environment for private activities. There is no *a priori* reason that privately offered recreational and social services competing with official agencies could not be partially financed or conducted in shared, underutilized buildings. The risk of over-regulation and political bias can never be eliminated but can, hopefully, be contained.

Nevertheless, the best-developed theories in social science cannot fully account for human preferences in allocating time and effort. It is certain, however, that when individuals no longer perceive value associated with organized activities or are unwilling to accept the discipline required for membership, social capital declines. We offer three possible explanations for the retreat from associations. First, potential participants have unrealistic expectations for what any private association can deliver. Second, preliminary meetings, directed by professional staff with a political or fundraising agenda, crowd out any personal reason for attending. Finally, organizations are perceived as being operated for and by an "inner-circle" and designed to exclude. Obvious solutions are transparency about what it is that an association seeks to deliver, fidelity to its unique mission, and openness to well-vetted initiatives consistent with that mission.

Tastes change, and future generation may revert to participation rather than spectator activities. The millennium cohort is a more connected generation, if only virtually through social media. In 2018, Deloitte International surveyed 10,455 college-educated full-time employees born between January 1983 and December 1994. Over 70 percent of these millennials find that their employers fail to support their desire to gain interpersonal skills, confidence, and ethics/integrity—that is, social capital. The perception that employers or governments are responsible for initiating social opportunities itself suggests a loss of social capital. To make a difference, young people need not wait for others to provide. A large degree of freedom to participate in and create new intermediaries remains.

It is possible that the next generation of Americans will dream big and fill the public square with coffee shops, restaurants, galleries, and a range of entrepreneurial activities. Included in this space, private schools, medical facilities, religious institutions, and social agencies will coexist with publicly sponsored ones. Children, the elderly, and those in between, protected by the rule of law and civil authorities, will cross paths as they go from music lessons to exercise classes, from scouting to square dancing, from great books clubs to fly-fishing. Whatever their socioeconomic circumstances, the lives of those initiating and assuming responsibilities for such activities will be enriched. In the process, they will experience the gamut of organizational complexity dealing with internalities and externalities, both positive and negative. This is how social capital is created.

References

Church Documents

All documents are available at www.vatican.va.

Pontifical Council for Justice and Peace, *Compendium of the Social Doctrine of the Church* (2004).

Catechism of the Catholic Church, Vatican City: Libreria Editrice Vaticana, 1994.

Second Vatican Council, *Gaudium et Spes* (Pastoral Constitution on the Church in the Modern World, 1965).

Pope John Paul II, Encyclical Letter *Centesimus Annus* (1991).

Pope John XXIII, Encyclical Letter *Mater Et Magistra* (1961).

Pope Leo XIII, Encyclical Letter *Rerum Novarum* (1891).

Books and Articles

Alesina, Alberto, and Paola Giuliano. "Culture and Institutions." *Journal of Economic Literature* 53, no. 4 (Fall 2015): 898–944.

Beito, David. "From Mutual Aid to the Welfare States: How Fraternal Societies Fought Poverty and Taught Character." Heritage Foundation, July 27, 2000, https://www.heritage.org/political-process/report/mutual-aid-welfare-state-how-fraternal-societies-fought-poverty-and-taught.

References

Costa, Dora L., and Matthew E. Kahn. *Heroes & Cowards: The Social Face of War*. Princeton: Princeton University Press, 2008.

Damon, William. *Stanford Civic Purpose Project: Longitudinal Study of Youth Civic Engagement in California, 2011–2013*. Ann Arbor: Inter-University Consortium for Political and Social Research, 2017, https://doi.org/10.3886/ICPSR36561.v1.

De Maeyer, Paul. "The Chinese 'Social Credit System': The Real Big Brother of the Future?" *Aleteia*, June 28, 2018, https://aleteia.org/2018/06/28/the-chinese-social-credit-system-the-real-big-brother-of-the-future/.

Fukuyama, Francis. "Social Capital: The Tanner Lectures on Human Values." Delivered at Brasenose College, Oxford, UK, May 12, 14, and 15, 1997. *University Reprints 2018*, 337–484, https://www.tannerlectures.utah.edu.

Hansmann, Henry B. "The Effect of Tax Exemption and Other Factors on the Market Share of Nonprofit Versus For-Profit Firms." *National Tax Journal* 40 (March 1987): 71–82.

Hayek, F. A. *The Road to Serfdom*. 1944; repr., Chicago: University of Chicago Press, 2007.

Horvarth, C. M. "Excellence versus Effectiveness: MacIntyre's Critique of Business." *Business Ethics Quarterly* 5, no. 3 (July 1995): 499–532.

Keating, Barry P., and Maryann O. Keating. *Microeconomics for Public Managers*. Chichester, UK: Wiley-Blackwell, 2009.

Levy, David M., and Sandra J. Peart. "Learning from Failure: A Review of Peter Schuck's *Why Government Fails So Often: And How It Can Do Better*." *Journal of Economic Literature* 53, no. 3 (2015): 667–74.

Machan, Tibor. *Initiative, Human Agency, and Society*. Stanford: Hoover Institution Press, 2000.

MacIntyre, Alasdair. *After Virtue: A Study in Moral Theory*, 2nd ed. Notre Dame: University of Notre Dame Press, 1984.

References

Meilaender, Gilbert. Review of Aladair MacIntyre. *Dependent Rational Animals: Why Human Beings Need the Virtues*, and *The MacIntyre Reader*. Edited by Kelvin Knight. *First Things*, October 1999, https://www.firstthings.com/article/1999/10/dependent-rational-animals-why-human-beings-need-the-virtues-and-the-macintyre-reader.

Murnane, Richard J., Sean F. Reardon, Preeya P. Mbekeani, and Anne Lamb. "Who Goes to Private School?" *Education Next* 18, no. 4 (2018), www.educationnext.org.

Murray, Charles. *Coming Apart: The State of White America, 1960–2010*. New York: Crown, 2012.

North, Douglas C., John Joseph Wallis, and Barry Weingast. "Violence and the Rise of Open-Access Orders." *Journal of Democracy* 20, no. 1 (January 2009): 55–68.

Putnam, Robert D. *Bowling Alone: The Collapse and Revival of American Community*. New York: Simon & Schuster, 2000.

Putnam, Robert D. "Tuning in, Tuning Out: The Strange Disappearance of Social Capital in America." *Political Science and Politics* 28, no. 4 (December 1995): 664–83.

Putnam, Robert D. *Our Kids: The American Dream in Crisis*. New York: Simon & Schuster, 2015.

Rupasingha, Anil, Stephan J. Goetz, and David Freshwater. "The Production of Social Capital in US Counties." *Journal of Socio-Economics* 35, no. 1 (2006): 83–101.

Reno, R. R. "False Freedom." *First Things*. October 2015, 3–7, https://www.firstthings.com/article/2015/10/false-freedom.

Schuck, Peter. *Why Government Fails So Often: And How It Can Do Better*. Cato Institute, April 13, 2014. Video, https://www.youtube.com/watch?v=N3YSFpOtUHs.

Smith, Vernon. *Constructivist and Ecological Rationality in Economics: Nobel Prize Lecture*. Fairfax, VA: Interdisciplinary Center for Economic Science. George Mason University, 2002.

References

Thomas, Clarence. "Victims and Heroes in the 'Benevolent State.'" In *Morality and Moral Controversies*. Edited by John Arthur. Upper Saddle River, NJ: Prentice Hall, 1999, 562–68.

Taranto, James. "What Went Wrong with Human Rights: A Weekend Interview with Aaron Rhodes." *Wall Street Journal*, August 18–19, 2018, A13.

United States Conference of Catholic Bishops. "Discrimination against Catholic Adoption Agencies." USCCB.org, http://www.usccb.org/issues-and-action/religious-liberty/discrimination-against-catholic-adoption-services.cfm.

Wolf Jr., Charles. "A Theory of Nonmarket Failure: Framework for Implementation Analysis." *Journal of Law & Economics* 22, no. 1 (1979): 107–39.

Zapatosky, Matt. "Justice Department Agrees to Settle Lawsuits over IRS Scrutiny of Tea Party Groups." *Washington Post*, October 25, 2017, https://www.washingtonpost.com/world/national-security/justice-department-agrees-to-settle-lawsuits-over-irs-scrutiny-of-tea-party-groups/2017/10/25/519513f8-b9f1-11e7-a908-a3470754bbb9_story.html.

About the Authors

MARYANN O. KEATING is a research fellow at the Indiana Policy Review Foundation. Born and raised in Philadelphia, she graduated from the University of Pennsylvania and studied on Fulbright at the Universidad Autónoma de Guadalajara, Mexico, and later at the University of Texas. She was then hired as an economist in the American Republics Division of the US Department of Commerce. Her PhD dissertation (University of Notre Dame, 1974) deals with the extent to which international capital flows affect the money supply process.

She has taught Principles of Economics and International Economics at several colleges in the United States and abroad. Her primary research focus evolved from macro to social economics. She edited Paul Samuelson's essays on *Economics from the Heart* (Thomas Horton and Daughters, 1983) and has co-authored several articles and books, including *Microeconomics for Public Managers* (Wiley-Blackwell, 2009).

BARRY P. KEATING has been Professor of Managerial Economics and Forecasting Analytics at the University of Notre Dame since 1978 and served as chair of the Department of Finance from 1991 to 1997. With Notre Dame, he has had opportunities to teach in London; Santiago, Chile; Freemantle, Western Australia; and China.

About the Authors

He received his MA from Lehigh University and his PhD from the University of Notre Dame in 1974. He then spent four years on the faculty at Virginia Tech, where he was fortunate enough to have James M. Buchanan and Gordon Tulloch assist him in putting together the pieces of economic theory. He is a member of the Philadelphia Society and a Heritage Fellow and has consulted for the Institute of Business Forecasting. He has published in professional journals and written several textbooks: *Business Forecasting and Analytics*, co-authored with Holt Wilson, is in its 7th edition. His hobbies include amateur radio (WD4MSM).

www.ingramcontent.com/pod-product-compliance
Lightning Source LLC
Chambersburg PA
CBHW071751080526
44588CB00013B/2214